T0366561

The Poems

THE SWISS LIST

ROBERT WALSER

The Poems

TRANSLATED BY
DANIELE PANTANO

LONDON NEW YORK CALCUTTA

Seagull Books, 2022

Originally published in volume form as *Die Gedichte*.
License edition by permission of the owner of rights,
the Robert Walser-Stiftung, Bern.

© Suhrkamp Verlag, Zürich, 1986

All rights reserved by and controlled through
Suhrkamp Verlag, Berlin.

First published in English translation by Seagull Books, 2022
English translation © Daniele Pantano, 2022

ISBN   978 1 8030 9 069 6

British Library Cataloguing-in-Publication Data
A catalogue record for this book is available
from the British Library.

Typeset by Seagull Books, Calcutta, India
Printed and bound in the USA by Versa Press

I would wish it on no one to be me.
Only I am capable of bearing myself.
To know so much, to have seen so much, and
To say nothing, just about nothing.

RW

CONTENTS

EARLY POEMS
(1897–1912)

Poems
(1909)

IN THE OFFICE

The moon peers in on us;
he sees me as a miserable clerk
langushing under the strict gaze
of my superior.
Embarrassed, I scratch my neck.
I have never known
life's lasting sunshine.
My flaw is my skill,
having to scratch my neck
under the gaze of my superior.

The moon is the wound of night,
every star a drop of blood.
Though far from the flower of luck,
I am made humble for it.
The moon is the wound of night.

YEARNING

I find it difficult
to laugh and joke.
What can I do?

In the weary heart,
the old suffering
maintains its course.

I must overcome
my habit of crying,
along with other things.

EVENING (I)

In the snow before me a path glimmers
black-yellow and goes on beneath the trees.
It is evening, and the air is heavy
and damp with colours.

The trees beneath which I walk
have branches like children's hands;
they plead without end,
ineffably kind, when I stand still.

Distant gardens and hedges
burn in a dark maze,
and the glowing sky, rigid with fear, sees
how the children's hands are reaching.

WINTER SUN

On house and garden walls,
it won't last long,
golden sunshine is burning.
Day has now lifted
what was woven in the countryside,
what was night and mist.
A comforting banging about,
expanding the chest, rubbing the hands,
blessed sunshine.
Now I too have forgotten
what weighed on me,
what was pain and suffering.

BUT WHY?

Now as such a clear
day came rushing back,
full of calm, genuine resolve,
he spoke slowly:
Now it shall be different,
I will join the battle;
like so many others,
I want to help rid the world of misery,
want to suffer and walk
until the people are free.
Never again shall I rest my tired head.
Something must
happen. Then a consideration caught up with him,
a nap: aw, just forget it.

MORNING STAR

I open the window,
a dark morning brightness.
The snow has already stopped,
a great star is in its place.

The star, the star
is wonderfully beautiful.
The distance all covered in snow,
covered in snow all the heights.

Holy and brisk,
the world's morning calm.
Each clear drop of sound;
the roofs glisten like children's tables.

So mute and white:
a great and beautiful solitude,
whose cold silence can be disturbed
by a mere utterance. It burns hot inside me.

PRAYER

Praying is the only
thing I will do tonight.
I have already achieved it,
I have kept awake for it,
this day, and now I can rest.

THE TREES (I)

(A Ballad)

They should not clench their fists,
it is my longing that is drawing near to them;
they should not stand there full of rage,
my longing is timidly drawing near to them;
they should not be ready to pounce like vicious dogs,
as if they wanted to tear my longing to shreds;
they should not threaten with broad sleeves,
that pains my longing.
Why have they suddenly changed?
As great and deep is my longing.
No matter how difficult, no matter how menacing:
I must reach them and I am already there.

WORLD (I)

There laugh, there rise
in the coming and going
of the world many deep worlds,
all wandering again
and fleeing through the others,
regarded as ever more beautiful.

They surrender in their orbits,
become large in their escape,
their vanishing is their existence.
I am no longer troubled,
for I can unpulverized strive
through the world as a world.

BRIGHTNESS

Grey days, on which
the sun carried itself
like a pale nun, are gone.
A blue day is blue above,
a world has freely risen
where sun and stars sparkle.

All of this transpired in silence,
without racket, as a great will,
and without much ceremony.
The miracle opens up smiling.
There is no need for rockets
or matches, only a clear night.

TO ROCK

I don't want to do much more
than stay awake a little longer.
It is so nice to be the only
one still awake and stirring.
I may as well lie down halfway
and while I fall asleep rock
myself already into a dream.

RUSHING

There is still this rush in the world,
the rush that never ceases.
I love—and it will never stop,
a love that rushes through the world.

And even though I am a coward,
and even though you are an invalid,
you love, though it is not you
who loves, I love, though it is not me.

It rushes, and I stand still, listening,
I know I hate that one and that one,
it is no use to me, no matter what I do:
I love everything, so that one, too.

Then there are times when I know
that for love we all burn.

NOT?

I lie in my room, tortured
by black memories.
How deeply I have been absent,
how I am forced to be absent.

Is the sun not shining today?
Surely all the poor rest
on their knees, with their warm
hearts, the fear on trembling faces.

Is the sun not shining today?

AS ALWAYS

The lamp is still here,
the table too is still here,
and I am still in this room,
and my longing, ah,
still sighs, as always.

Cowardice, are you still here?
And Lie, you, too?
I hear a dark Yes:
Misfortune is still here,
and I am still in this room,
as always.

DEEP WINTER

In the windowpanes are buried
those infinitely fond, frail
flowers, like a giant tear
the yellow moon hangs in a nebular garden.

The world is a garden where
all delights have now died,
and sound and heaven are spoiled.
The window flowers are the frozen mind.

On the many white rooftops,
on the fields that are just as white,
the moon weeps, even in rooms
where people are mad or wise.

SNOW (I)

It is snowing, it is snowing, it covers
the world with white trouble, so far, so far.

The flakes are swirling so painfully
from the sky, the snow, the snow.

Ah, it gives you a sense of calm, a vastness,
the snow-covered world makes me weak.

Thus small at first, and then large my
longing presses me to tears from within.

FEAR (I)

I wish
the houses would move,
come after me,
that would be frightening.

I wish
my heart would twist,
and my mind stop,
that would be frightening.

The most frightful I wish
to press against my heart.
I long for fear,
for pain.

SHEPHERD'S TRYST

Here it is quiet, here it feels good,
here the meadows are fresh and pure,
and a spot in shade and sunshine
like well-behaved children.
Here the strong desire
that is my life dissolves,
I no longer know desire,
here my will dissolves.
I am so still, so warmly moved,
lines draw through my emotions,
I don't know, it is all confused,
yet everything has been proven wrong.
I no longer hear any complaints,
yet there is complaining in the room
of such a soft kind, so white, so dreamy,
and again I am left knowing nothing.
I only know that it is quiet here,
stripped of all needs and doings,
here it feels good, here I can rest,
for no time measures my time.

RETURNING HOME (I)

My cheeks are red hot,
my lip still trembles,
because I sent my heart
to speak; every word of it
delusional and awkward,
an exuberance, an abrupt sound.
That's how I spoke, oh, it still
shows on my hot cheeks
I am now carrying home.
I look down at the snow
and walk past many houses,
past many hedges, many trees,
the snow adorns hedge, tree and house.
I walk on, staring down
at the snow, on my cheeks
nothing but red-hot memory
reminding me of my wild talk.

SILENCE

How happy I would be, if I could
just rest somewhere in peace,
if happiness, like a warm dress,
would grant me inner silence.

How I would love to somehow
find some solace in it,
which is all but certain,
for it puts an end to all strife.

ONWARDS

I wanted to stand still,
I urged myself further,
past black trees,
but beneath black trees,
I wanted to suddenly stand still,
I urged myself further,
past green meadows,
but next to those green meadows,
I only wanted to stand still,
I urged myself further,
past needy little cottages,
beside one of those cottages,
I really want to stand still,
regarding its need,
and how the smoke gently
rises into the sky, I would
like to stand still now awhile.
That's what I said and laughed,
the green of the meadows laughed,
the smoke rose smiling like smoke,
I urged myself further.

SIN

I see how they glow,
the night and morning dews,
the heated meadows.
I see the blinding sun,
I sit among wall after
wall, it is a sin.

Bright shadows
are walking through
unsettled pastures
now colourful panels.
I sit trapped by anger
and fear, it is a crime.

IN THE MOONLIGHT

Last night I thought
the stars were singing,
as I woke up
and heard a soft sound.

But it was a lyre drifting
through the rooms,
such an anxious sound
in the cold, sharp night.

I thought about failed
efforts, prayers and curses,
and for a while I heard it singing,
lay awake for quite a while.

A LITTLE LANDSCAPE

There is a little tree in the meadowland
and many more good little trees there too.
A little leaf freezes in the frosty wind
and many lone little leaves there too.
A little pile of snow shimmers at the edge of a brook
and many more little white piles there too.
A little mountain peak laughs into the bedrock
and many more impish peaks there too.
And in the middle of it all stands the Devil
and still more poor devils there too.
A little angel turns away his weeping face
and all the angels in heaven there too.

WITH A WEEPING HEART

I feel a thousand things when
I think of you, Jesus.
It burns inside me, for
your name is a bewildering kiss.

You are still standing in the snow
and stare, something the poor ask,
the poor, who are said to have
caused you such harm.

But it was not their doing,
the horror of your death,
those left alone, no, never!
It was a pig-headed drunkard.

It was done by ruffians
full of debauchery.
Poverty has nothing in common
with the source of your blood, nothing.

I will have understood
poverty as a quiet pain,
people, outside the bonds
of the deed, scattered, soft, like snow.

And they stare brightly like him,
as Jesus watches them,
to this day his light blonde
curls flutter without rest.

From time to time it happens
that Jesus smiles once more,
tender and with a wonderful spirit
and soothing like the night.

And in the morning all that is left
are his footprints in the snow.
He belongs to the poor, those who are
said to have caused him such harm.

AT THE WINDOW (I)

The heart-warm brown of the earth,
the childlike white upon it,
the silver-green meadow now
have brought a dream into the world,
the dream of smiles.

The hand of a kind person
is stroking my cheek,
my eye is blessedly blind,
otherwise I would be able to tell
whose hands are so tender.

The dream of happy smiles
has been brought into the world
by womanly and delicate colours
that nod approvingly,
I am now standing at the window.

PUT ASIDE

I make my way;
it goes on a bit
and homeward; then without sound
or word, I am put aside.

BEFORE GOING TO SLEEP

As it has been granted yet again,
as the world is in its blackest rest,
I will do nothing else,
except to joyfully open
the longing veiled by day.

TOO PHILOSOPHICAL

How ghostly my life
in its fall and rise.
Always I see myself waving to myself,
floating away from the one waving.

I see myself as laughter,
as deep mourning again,
as a wild weaver of talk;
but all this falls away.

And all this time it has
never been quite right.
I have been chosen to
wander forgotten distances.

BOY'S LOVE

The pretty girl came in passing,
he knelt, as she came slowly,
he knelt, and he sang to her
a song with string music;
he played for her his true love,
with melancholy and a smile;
shy his heart rang amid the string music,
which trembling sounded like love,
his eyes beheld the girl,
his teeth shimmered in his mouth,
with which he sang, shaking, pleading.
The love song did not end;
infinite, like his love, the warm
strains came from him.
Thus did he recite his desire,
the air billowed with love and import,
the blue sky looked down on them,
but the girl ran away,
she disappeared, and then
the soft strains of love perished too.

DISAPPOINTMENT

You never forget disappointment,
as the siren call of happiness is unforgettable.
To remember is to yearn, oh, yearning,
as it is so immeasurable,
you will never forget it.

OPPRESSIVE LIGHT

Two trees stand in the snow,
the sky, tired of light,
returns home, and nothing other
than gloom close by.

And beyond the trees
dark houses tower up.
Now you hear something said,
now dogs begin to bay.

Now the dear, round lamp-
moon appears in the house.
Now the light goes out again,
the way a wound gapes.

How small life is here
and how big nothingness.
The sky, tired of light,
has given everything to the snow.

The two trees bow
their heads to each other.
Clouds traverse the world's
silence in a circle dance.

EASIER SAID

May the hours stretch
like the sky and my yearning.
Fast like the naming of a name
is my flying recognition.
Faster than the swelling hours,
faster than desire's pleading
is my overcoming the pressure.

AFRAID

I have waited so long for sweet
talk and greetings, just one sound.

Now I am afraid; no talk or sound,
only an abundance of fog setting in.

Whatever sang and hid in dark ambush:
Misery, sweeten now my grave path.

DO YOU SEE?

Do you see me crossing the meadows
that are stiff and dead from the fog?
I long for that home,
that home I have never had,
and without any hope
that I will ever be able to reach it.
For such a home, never touched,
I carry that longing that will
never die, like this meadow here dies,
which is stiff and dead from the fog.
You do see me crossing it, full of dread?

AND LEFT

He quietly waved his hat
and left, they say of the wayfarer.
It tore the leaves off a tree
and left, they say of the bleak autumn.
Smiling, she dealt out favours
and left, they say of her Majesty.
At night it knocked on the door
and left, they say of heartbreak.
Crying, he pointed at his heart
and left, they say of the poor man.

HOUR

The hour comes, the hour goes;
there is so much in an hour,
the back-and-forth of emotions,
the longing that blows like a morning breeze.
The day says its prayers
and curses in an hour,
and I am always the poor house
filled with cheers or laments.
The world lies inside an hour,
unaware, not needing anything,
and, ha, I do not always know
where it rests and sleeps, my world.

WEARINESS

Carry me off as I am;
see, my lost mind
rejects this world
that clarifies nothing now.

Come to me, oh, I will
be good and blissfully calm
in your dense glow,
holy, sweet sleep.

ILLUSION

Again tired hands,
again tired legs,
an incessant darkness,
I laugh the walls
into spinning, but this is
a lie, because I am crying.

SERENITY

Ever since I surrendered myself to time,
I feel something alive inside me,
warm, marvellous tranquillity.
Ever since I chaffed the days
and the hours head-on,
my complaints are locked away.

And I am relieved of my burden,
of my debts that cause me harm,
by a plain-spoken expression:
Time is time, it may pass away,
but it will always find me again,
this good person by the old spot.

String and Desire

WINTER NIGHT

The moon is shining on the snow.
A bright night in the sky.
The stars have just awoken.
The world glistens white and pure.

Leaning against the window, I look
at the sky, which is flashing
with stars, longing grips
my heart, which longs afresh.

IT IS NIGHT

It is night, and there is the glow
of a lamp in my room.
It is night, and there is the pain
of worry in my heart.
It is night, and there is the bliss
of courtly love on my mind.

ROMANCE

Oh, like roses they
tossed me glances,
the two girls.
I feigned rest.

Was the world so red
or was it my blushing?
Burning whispers
shuddered around me.

What did I do—dug my hands
deep into my trouser pockets.
A swift over with must first
stir me from the embers.

I did not look back.
I just thought, how
like roses their glances
shook the restless one.

TIME

I lie here, I do have time,
I ponder here, I do have time.
The day is dark, it has time,
more time than I wish for, time
I shall measure, for a long time.
Time grows with the passing of time.
Only one thing transcends time,
and that's longing, no time is on time
when it comes to longing's time.

MEADOW GREEN

A lovely meadow
green has emerged
from the melted snow,
a green, a dark green.
The same appears to the world
as a mild sun now,
as a wild sun now,
as a warm sun now.
For the real one doesn't shine,
the real one doesn't warm.
For the real one is gone.
Thick clouds cover
its glow the world
doesn't miss anyway,
because the dark meadow
green from melted snow
appears as a sun to the world.
As a sun it warms the world,
as a sun it spangles the world:
this green that has emerged.

EVENING (II)

Not only in the sky is
there a vast evening grey.
In the wide world as well
is a vast evening grey.
The snow is evening silent.
The green is evening lovely,
the trees all likewise,
the houses all likewise.
And smoke rises from
the houses into evening air
filled with happiness for me.
My happiness is an evening happiness.

AT THE WINDOW (II)

By the window I see out,
it is so lovely outside,
there is not much out there.
There is a little snow
on which it rains now.
There is a creeping green
that creeps into the darkness.
That darkness is the night,
which will soon cover the world,
it will cover all the snow,
it will cover all the green.
This kind green creeping
into darkness; oh how lovely.
From the window I see this.

EVERYTHING GREEN

Gently the meadows draw out,
take up this calm green
and bring it back,
this green, soon it is near,
soon again it is far,
so far that my fear,
my longing stir inside me.
And a longing is dead after all
and a terror is dead after all.
Gently the meadows draw
the dead fear out
of my heart, then
everything is still again.
And I see all the world
filled by beautiful meadows.
Wherever I look, too,
filled by green meadows,
and only with green, with a green
that remains unfailingly still,
is the whole world full.

THE BELOVED

I lift the curtain:
I see the golden sun
shining on green meadows.
I see the blue sky
shining on green meadows.
I see sun and sky
laughing on green meadows.
I lower the curtain
and look around the room.
The room is full of sun.
The room is full of sky.
How beautiful is this, my beloved!
I speak and I laugh:
My room is a sky.
How I love the sky.
How beautiful is this, my beloved!

SNOW (II)

Now all I see of the world,
of the sky and the earth,
is nothing but white snow.
Here snow and more snow,
there snow and more snow.
I see nothing of the green
but a stretch of snow.
I see nothing of the blue
but an expanse of snow.
The world is all white now.
The world is dead.
The world is gone.
As it was before,
it rushes inside me:
there a haunting green squalls,
there a soft blue wells up
inside me from far-reaching snow,
I stand still with a beating heart
in the room, ah, so this is
a world full of green now,
a world full of blue now.

THUS IT FALLS THROUGH THE TREES

Thus it falls through the trees,
thus it falls on the meadow,
now a world of snow
and turns the world to snow.
Thus it lies on the rooftops,
thus it lies in the distance,
now this something soft, dear,
now deep, deep snow.

FLOWERS

I yearn for the first bouquet of flowers,
for the bouquet of flowers that smells
like a life without worries.
It can't be soon, for winter
still grips the meadow
that offers bouquets, but my longing
already picks a hundred thousand flowers.
How they smell, how they all
tease the small and tender creatures
in my soul—bouquets of flowers
are now the yearning in my soul.

WINTER RAIN

I see soft rain
falling on hard meadows,
falling on fierce trees,
falling on dark houses,
from a frantic sky,
on the dormant earth
that fell asleep in winter.
This shall change now.
The earth shall wake,
the meadows shall rise,
the trees shall gently behold
the familiar houses,
for a gentle, mild rain
from a frantic sky
visits the winter earth.

ALL IS NIGHT

Day is now night,
for it is full of rain.
The snow was a bright day
and the cold a bright day.
Rain is night.
A day full of rain
is also a night.
The snow was such a bright day.
The nice day was dressed
in snow and cold.
Day without snow is night.
Now the rainy night turns
the entire world into night,
turns me into grave night too.

FEAR (II)

In this bright and silent room
soft voices crush
my heart into a wallow of dreams.
O I have never heard
the magic sound bathe
so deeply in my emotions.

Yet a wonderful rush
and a spirit-pounding tremor
still and always pierces my
overfearful eavesdropping
and turns into an anguished life
in this bright and silent room.

VOICES

In my ears
there is a lost,
tender hiss,
a distant rush.

Inside me
a memory
of lovely hours
vanished now.

My eyes tremble,
I am crying because
of the soft singing,
of the sweet sound.

Letting go of the gentle,
pale voices of the heart
covered in darkness
is what I strive for now.

DIFFICULT MORNING

In a hot, rumpled bed
I spent a long night,
and, oh, how I am
afraid even out of bed.

Sadly I prepare myself
to face the difficult path of life,
and I fight the sweet urge for
solace, what good is it anyway.

You need to control yourself, overcome,
no matter how difficult it may seem,
or how strongly desire braces itself
against caressing, comforting sounds.

FEVER

My heart beats
such relief, relief.
The evening sets heavy
with darkness and healing.

There storms above me
inexpressible gratitude.
Hope climbs
and stirs;

I let it flatter
the heart and
caress my burning
wound that remains.

HOPE

How long it extracts itself
from its small, quiet confinement,
hope, for days on end.
Always it knows how to twist,
how to find a small hole
through which it can slip.
My heart has so many weaknesses,
it tries for days on end
to talk them all away.
How can its humiliating
restrain my mocking,
which cuts so deep.

UNDER A GREY SKY

Under a grey sky,
under a heavy sky,
there is a small white house.
Inside the small white house,
in this little room,
I sit sad.

Through leafless trees,
through wet trees,
my eye searches and sees,
finds poor meadows.
On behalf of these meadows
I cry bitterly.

ALL THIS

All this talk about vast space
turns bit by bit into more than a dream.

Oh, how I wish I were a small tree
standing by the edge of a little brook.

EVENING SONG

There are only a few people still walking around,
now there is one left, and then they are all gone.

Something like the weariness of nature
wants to lie down on the houses and fields.

It smiles so subtly from tree to tree,
but you can barely recognize the smile.

How miserable is the small breeze
that still travels the evening world.

I begin to feel hesitant and tired;
I consider only the gravest of men,

the Moon, who grows more important,
as soon as the sun breaks free from the earth.

PEACE?

I walk back and forth up there
and look at the mountains.

It is so quiet, so peacefully quiet,
the air and me and the earth are quiet.

There is a beautiful forest before me.
How long and well I know this forest!

There is also a small house before me,
a tavern, or a farmhouse;

it lies so quietly like the whole world
and the trees stand so quietly in the world.

I suppose I should move on,
I must leave peace and quiet.

THE FOREST (I)

I entered this forest
and now I cannot leave.
It is over with my peace.
I entered this forest.
I stare: how beautiful is this forest!
In it the sunshine hangs yellow.
My mind and feelings have been stirred.
Is this forest really this beautiful, this beautiful?
The whole world is dead to me now,
because there is no other place left but this
that still breathes; my senses' trickery
has killed the whole world for me now.
But each rock and each trunk
in this forest are most dear to me.
I will never return to you,
my beloved, in this other world.
I am in love with this forest,
my heart has been cut into a thousand pieces,
it wanders around, it gets caught
on it all, because it is in love with it all.
How the entire world is dead to me!
I cannot say what I feel, I am too shy,
but given the guile of my sensibilities,
the world is dead to me, except here.

BEER SCENE

One man frolicked with the waitress.
One man propped his tired head up.
One man played the piano soulfully.
One man's laughter burst from his mouth.
One man's dream was shot by darkness.
One man's stiff key yielded.
Once the slender girl ran away.
Once the stupid dreamer woke.
Once the music was an English song.
A coquetted chatterbox, tobacco smoke,
a woken dreamer, and a dream,
a tired piano virtuoso.

WHITE LAUNDRY

The white laundry stirs quietly
in the garden, in the gentle breeze
that blows whimsically from the sky.
The sky is half still, half wild;
it drifts halfway into the clouds,
it peeks boldly halfway through the blue.
The sun has already been forgotten
and the world readies itself
to set in a garden,
the evening; white laundry is blowing
in the evening and in the gentle breeze,
in the evening wind. Does something
inside me also stir like billowing laundry?
I do not believe it, the calm night
is already completely in charge here.
A tiny breeze no longer stirs inside me.

ON MY MIND

I have not slept for many nights
because of my wandering's greed.

> On my mind,
> abused, wounded,
> falls darkness now.
> I look inward.

ABOUT THE FOREST

Its ground is soft like a carpet,
its air is soothing like a balm,
its voice is the sound of a song,
plain and slender like its trunks' growth.
Its voice is the sound of love.
Each morning I hark and listen
in the green riddle of its dwelling.
Each morning I see my eyes,
in love, its silent miracle,
its wounds, for soon it will be dead.—
Red blood streams from the trunks—
its wounds, for soon it will be dead.

FORGOTTEN

I already forgot the forgotten.
The half-forgotten gently tortures me.
It rises up with its love
and frets in the circle of thoughts,
like an impatient hand
rummaging in a work basket,
as it could not find the right thing
and now keenly feels this affliction.
So comes shy and pale again
what I already half forgot.
Thus lives what I had already laid to rest,
again and again, for it bears life.

LOVE

I am my own sweetheart.
It is me who loves and hates me.
Ah, no power of love seizes
me as completely as myself.
Often, when I lay for hours
deep in thought with myself,
I was my night, I was my day,
I was my anguish and sunshine.
I am the sun that warms me.
I am the heart that loves me,
that carried away devotes itself,
that pines for its sweetheart.

FOG

Anxiously I watch
the fog return from
the deep river gorge.
How it displaces the blue,
how its rushing greed
narrows the bright ray of light.
Oh, that the sun must go,
that once blindingly bright,
it must fade yet again.
To rid myself of heavy
thoughts, I send my
greetings and the sun's kiss.

Further Selections

THE FUTURE!

A beautiful time is coming
when the royal halls of kings
will echo with a new belief
in freedom on their marble.

When a nation will walk in love
up and down the avenues;
when unrestraint progress shall bloom—
and a thousand songs blossom!

When people will be but people
and love each other without end,
and when the work that weeps now
will be turned into the greatest pleasure.—

When passion and noble deeds
share a profound relationship.
The happiness of an era of freedom
will be expressed by a free race!

A beautiful time is coming,
of which we shall sing songs.— —
I hear already the golden eagle's
'spirit' boldly flapping its wings.

FOR MY DARLING FANNY!

Never look the other way in life,
always take part in the fight,
seize it and battle your way through,
then you will have your inner peace.

Have no doubts or suspicious looks
and never indulge in a shy moment.
Have faith in your God and be proud
and smart in every dire situation.

GLOOMY NEIGHBOUR

It does sit there just like any other house,
but all day long the screaming
of poor children leaks out.
The children of 'better' people
are seized quickly by the ears, quickly,
and the poor ones twice as fast.
Oh that spite must now add
its foot to misery and despair,
that all the poor have already
been chosen as hate's first victims.

It does sit there just like any other house,
but all day long the crying
of poor children leaks out.

DREAMS

Turbid dreams sped
through my sleep, and
thus spoiled my sleep.
Now the shapes of night
can no longer hold on,
because morning has struck.

How gloomy this morning,
already the day's worries
are crowding out the day,

which, above all else,
will bring me calm,
no matter what it will bring.

CLOSING TIME

After a spent day, I
walked back home in a fever.
The whole way home
the sun touched my cheeks.

The blissful evening glow
spread across the meadows
and I called this light
the blood I shed.

My hot burning blood lay
consoling the entire world.
So I walked with pride—
now that all was tilled.

I did not know what was happening,
I leaned against a fence post,
in my blood that covered
the meadows near and far.

LAUGHING AND SMILING

I feel like laughing
and smiling.
What does it matter!
Things are like that . . .

FOR FANNY

No, I am done groaning,
careless pleasures shall
be at my service again.

Oh, how nice to have servants,
to feast on the thought
of being a beloved master.

FAINT-HEARTED

Silent grief
visited me,
I descended
into its awe,

I felt there
not fear, not haste,
only a heavy burden.
Grief then led me

further on
through a dark sorrow,
until the strider
returned to the light.

I bade softly:
Keep me—
but it moved on
to a new journey.

TRAGEDY

The curtain rises to a serious height:
the play appears, and the piece begins.
The men make proud warrior faces,
twisting their mouths into evil grins
that promise death, already wounds burst
open and blood stains their pale brows rose.
The determined to die slits open his belly.
His son screams outside the door, the door
collapses, and, as if turned to stone, he watches
the gruesome sight—he was too late.
The scene changes, and the eye peers
into a garden's dream: the man
emerges, colossally magnified and terribly
changed, from the dark bushes,
deliberate and limber; and a black
cloak flaps like a spectre around his limbs,
which measure the sweeping tragic steps
on the parquet floor of the stage. Then a fight,
a struggle that makes angry bones crack.
One of them falls, trips like a small bird
until he tumbles horribly. The other
must flee, but they bring him back a prisoner
and announce the intended judgment.
The little girl is to blame for all of this,
she who just barely learned to smile
with reason. As sweet as sin, innocent yet
already skilled in the art of guilt, she
steps forth as a bright light, tossing charm
and horror into the minds of the anxious audience.
Mourning after her, a torch goes out.

THE CONCERTINA PLAYER

This morning the concertina player
just starts playing once more;
it is bright and cold outside,
the day looks wide-eyed.

No less as concerned he plays,
as yesterday, when it was night,
when it filled the rooms,
shy, kind, nameless.

He will surely play all day
as the best way to forget
his past and future trials.
The tokens of fate!

I WANDERED

I wandered and wander still,
though my walking was not always the same.
Soon I brought cheerfulness with me.
Soon, and the same is true for the sky,
my desire suddenly lost itself
in a long day of suffering—

POEMS WRITTEN IN BIEL
(1919–1920)

SPRING (I)

Surely everyone is happy that it is warm
again, and that the windows are open,
that a spring wind blows into the room.
Presumably no one resents
that the woods are greening again,
that meadows are full of grass,
that birds are singing in the trees,
that violets are blooming from the earth.
Hundreds and thousands of green leaves!
Spring is a field marshal
who conquers the world,
and no one holds a grudge.
A victorious sea of blossoms
drifts across the lands. The regions
are white, as though a princess
were about to arrive. Oh,
everything is so tenuous,
too tenuous to last.
But what foolish talk; spring is
brief, everyone knows that.
A child's play in the open!
'Is it possible?' people wonder
and look at each other and smile. One
even cries with joy. It is difficult
to face all this glory and not be
moved. Though spring has been here
before, time and time again
it is new and always youthful.
The old walks with the young. Husband
with wife. The small with the great,
and all are made brothers: nations

with nations. The lover sneaks
to his beloved. He sings. Only he
who truly loves achieves a song.
Kissing and dreaming.—Nearby,
with a sinister face, life's gravity
is standing by a wall; and whoever
walks past it, must tremble.

SULKING

One of Keller's novels,
and you will know this,
is about Pankraz, the Sulker,
who roved all over the world,
until one day a lion finally
cured him of his vanity.
It was surely no mere
coincidence that the poet
wrote about this topic.
No, there is no doubt
that he intentionally
mocked such a burden.
To sulk is a grave mistake,
how much unpleasantness
has it caused already.
Many believe sulking
is a sign of character,
but this cannot be the case.
He who sulks is a poor churl
and servant to his own bad habit,
paying tribute to the rule of trouble.
Sulking has everything do with
narcissism and with an always apparent
and deeply injured sense of pride.
No one is able to
refute such a sentence,
rather, one will attest to it.
Sulking is not difficult to learn,
there are too many people
who have mastered it already.
All of Keller's characters

are significant in their own way;
we do enjoy a sulking figure.
Sulking is something truly wicked,
it has probably always been with us,
flourishing throughout the ages.
He who wastes his time sulking
is truly incapable of claiming
that he is doing something useful.
So far I have mostly spoken in prose,
today, however, with your permission,
I speak in festive verse.
Sulking is a sign of pettiness,
are you willing to surrender yourself
in shame to such a weakness?
You can watch how even intelligent
people now and again fall only too
quickly into the abyss of sulking.
No one has yet benefitted
much from sulking;
you can trust me on that.
Women enjoy sulking because
of unrequited feelings,
artists because of being ignored.
In the political click and clack,
as in our small private lives,
we often sulk about adversities.
Away with all this sulking, for it
is everything but a treat
and only spoils our lives.
He who fights a fairly honest
battle with himself can
tame and defeat this evil.
Only through acceptance and
kind forgiveness, not anger,

can you show courage.
Oh, be kind, not hostile,
gentle and strong and happy and free,
faithful, brave and patient.
Go on and look forward,
think about how short life is,
thus you will never sulk again.
I do not have to say anything else,
for whatever I might add
will ultimately speak for itself.

LITTLE MOUSE

The other day, when I saw a dead
mouse in the middle of my way,
I stood still and said: What is this?
Why do you lie here so quietly?
Having barely entered this life,
you are already fleeing from it.
Well, let me at least consider
the jolly path your life has taken:
There were certainly no words
wasted when you arrived here,
a baptism was probably a waste.
You never went to school,
no teachers were ever forced to work
themselves to death over you.
You knew from the first day
how to find your place in this life.
When it came to your upbringing,
higher studies, knowledge, awareness,
you were free to do without all that.
You never had any piano lessons,
dancing lessons, gymnastics
lessons or other kind of lesson.
You were born with grace
and agility and an entirely
natural sense of decency.
Shoes, socks, hat and gloves
remained unknown to you.
You always wore the same suit.
Did you have any brothers and sisters,
uncles, aunts and cousins?
Were you by any chance married?

These are questions we all rather
not ask in the end because
they are all too complicated.
Of course, my dear mouse,
you never had to care about anything.
Our kind is full of doubts;
we convince ourselves of God knows,
we make our time on this earth
as annoying as possible;
we struggle and wear ourselves down,
we seemingly go mad with all
those delicate worries of ours.
It is obvious that you were
very happy just to be alive,
you had hardly any worries at all,
which make you, in almost all cases,
nothing but frustrated anyway.
I doubt I am very much mistaken,
when I think about how you loved
to squeeze through small crevices.
A small quantity of leaves
was the world in which you lived,
you liked to crawl under rocks.
When we humans see a bit of grass,
you must see something quite large.
Trees, oak trees, for example,
must have seemed colossal to you,
if you were ever able to overlook
such girth and such grandness.
Even a hare must have seemed
rather respectable to you.
Yet you were especially afraid
of cats, so much that you avoided
even the slightest chance of trouble.

Your voice was a whistling,
and your walk was like a dart.
You could not speak German,
nor French or English,
you clung to your Mouselish,
it was enough to be able
to talk to your own kind.
You did not create any kind
of important work in your life.
You never had a need to travel.
This makes you no less
important in the eyes of our
Father up there in the clouds,
which floated above you as well
as any other beings on earth.
So goodbye.—And when I had
said all this, I continued walking.

RETURNING HOME (II)

If I allowed myself
to jabber about the past,
I would honestly say: It was
seemingly absolutely not bad.
I was often allowed to mingle
with a lot of nice people.
I lived in a very fine house
with the kindest of women,
let myself be spoiled no end.
Every day we ate fresh eggs,
butter, cheese, succulent ham, all
I had to do was boldly help myself.
Thus worries I had very few,
or no worries at all,
I was the grand lord.
I wrote droll little love
letters with a golden quill
and took a leisurely walk through
the garden whenever I felt like it,
where beautiful flowers grew
in the shade of shrubberies,
or strolled at will through
I do not know how many rooms,
one lovelier than the next.
Yes, I lived quite the lazy life,
a cushier one could not be imagined,
a more charming one not be dreamt.
My dear wife almost withered
away with affection for me,
always called me her darling,
wrapped her arms around my neck,

pulled gently on my earlobe and
a hundred other such things.
In the evenings I listened to music,
at noon I was defenceless against
the most pleasant slumber.
At five o'clock I enjoyed my teatime,
smoked French tobacco,
covered myself in clouds of smoke,
lay on a luxurious daybed
and dispelled my boredom
with some enthralling reading.
Outside the window, which I
carefully covered with mantles,
nightingales were piping up.
Girls looked like violets,
the moon like a gentle sun,
the bright day like midnight.
Life resembled a dark forest,
the earth a beautiful dancer,
and eternity was like the sea.
Spring had golden leaves,
lips were red like roses.
My hands were much too soft
for me to consider them
capable of hard work.
I picked an elegant suit
to flap around my limbs,
on my head sat a top hat.
Whenever I felt like it,
I easily mixed with people.
In that gracefully tumultuous,
cheerfully chaotic ebb and flow,
the myriad fellowships,
I bathed in true bliss.

But as nice as it all was,
and no matter the delight
and spirit I undoubtedly felt,
I longed for something else entirely.
What is the rush of pleasure
compared to happiness?
All kinds of changes reminded
me more urgently than ever
to settle for something honest.
A stay in my homeland seemed
to me the most beautiful choice.
I wanted to see mountains again,
listen to plain and modest words.
All I had experienced up until then
faded away, as if it were a dream,
and thus one day I decided
to leave and go back home.
O, how happy I was about it.

DOLL

Please look at me for once,
do you not find me dignified?
I am a doll, I have very
interesting eyes that are
only made of glass and thus
are not good for much.
My limbs are full of sawdust.
Walking is simply impossible,
sitting works somewhat better,
and I am very good at lying down.
I have never done any work,
my hands are way too stiff,
my lips remain forever sealed,
they have never uttered a word,
my voice has never been heard.
Dolls are silent like fish.
I cannot laugh or cry.
Pain and joy, hate and love
I let people deal with,
who as we know get
emotional only too quickly.
I am always at the mercy
of some kind of change,
I am never frightened,
nothing unsettles me,
I feel, think, sense nothing
at all and I am apathetic
quite in the extreme.
To startle dolls out of their
sleep is hardly possible.
You see me constantly

making the same strange face.
I have never had a soul,
affection is utterly alien to me,
I am a sort of phenomenon
when it comes to immutability,
what a disgraceful confession!
Is a doll a doll
because of its liveliness?
I am based on, maintained
by illusion, simple as that.
Children appreciate me;
to them I am in every way
more than welcome as a plaything,
they can busy themselves with me,
because they have imagination.
Adults, on the other hand,
most certainly feel that
they are superior to me.
There is a reason for this,
of course, as I am generally
speaking unbelievably unhelpful.
To act on my own is something
that would never cross my mind,
I am utterly dependent
on the support of others.
There is plenty of evidence
that I am unusually
lifeless, stiff and dry.
To a child's mind, however,
I am absolutely alive,
I eat, drink, go on walks,
lie down in bed just like a real person
and charm them with my talk;
and all this is only imagined,

and can easily add this
and that imaginary thing.
O, the little ones are so much
smarter than the big ones think.
It is they who know how to live.

THE KIND

So, are the kind all dead already?
No, no, they are still alive, I know
it for a fact, my little finger tells me;
but I think they are scattered far
and wide, like blossoms carried
by the wind and tossed around
like waves.—Is it so? I could be
mistaken, and how I wish I were
wrong. One here, the other there,
and all of them lonely, all of them
abandoned, because there is no
longer a bond? What sort of picture
am I painting here, one that will
not make me happy, or excite you?
But it is certainly not so, they are all
living together, are all united in the
friendliest way, hold hands and look
at each other, and above them
are pretty, white, lovely clouds
and a clear, fresh blue floats up there,
and winds blow against their
brows, which think and imagine
such wonderful things, and their hearts
are calm, and their noble souls filled
with an everlasting patience, and
their surroundings are green, and
the place is holy. Day and night
are like siblings, the sun and moon
like lovers, and everything, everything
is friendly. Plants have eyes, talk
like people, and the latter resemble

the intimacy and quiet prosperity
of flowers. But where is this?
What is the name of this country?
How can we find it? Just look in front
of you, that is how you will see it, for
the kind still live all around us, and those
who have it within themselves will feel beauty.

CHOPIN

How lovely it is to listen to him,
he immediately lets you dream
and fantasize. If you have never
been in love, now you are a
lover and no longer belong to
yourself, and you rejoice.
O what bliss to no longer
think about the poor self,
to feel rich, because all of your
emotions have been freed from
the constricting and common self.
Chopin's music, is it a lock of hair,
is it a seductive smile,
the smell of Egyptian cigarettes,
the shape and scent of flowers? O, how
the heart now blooms and revels in the soul.
A wonderful, golden abyss opens
in front of you, and the evening sun
caresses you, and you are in a different
land, where things are much
more delicate and soft,
and calm and free,
where tall trees wrap you in shade
and light and darkness blend
into lovely melodies,
where grief is beautiful and
melancholy blissful, just like
the music of this Pole, who once
gave concerts in Paris, where he played
for the whole world, for soldiers,
simple workers, for bankers, ministers.

Whose admiration did he not arouse
with the flirting of his hands?
He cast a spell on everyone. Heinrich
Heine, the mocker, loved and honoured him.
He played as if he performed only for
himself, society and loneliness
were all the same for him, yet
his most intimate he revealed
in the midst of the world's crowd,
that is why he played so beautifully,
because sharing it made him happy.
Giving is a need for any noble spirit.

SUNDAY

Six weekdays have passed,
today you rest from work,
the sun is shining, which goes
without saying on a Sunday.
You get up a little later
and put on your nicest clothes,
then you might go on a walk
and chat with a few acquaintances.
Sunday has a delicate, lovely,
noble, soothing face,
like a child's golden curls
and dreamy, blue eyes,
hands that seek to caress you
and lips that speak to your soul
of everything beautiful and dear.
The food is especially good,
the good mood extra joyful,
and a jauntiness that soaks you
practically from head to toe.
You like to spend the afternoon
outdoors, that is for sure,
in pleasantly eventful circles,
with polite and good people,
for nothing compares to cheerful
company and friendly interaction.
You lie in the grass and in the
welcome shade of tall, ancient trees,
and you feel Sunday's peace
within and around you, you
jest and indulge in the banter
of others and laugh about it.

Good company is like the sun,
unselfish, affectionate,
brave in the loving sense, for
love is above all else, villages,
cities and countries, and lakes
and rivers, and the distant oceans
and our human struggle,
everything is gloriously connected.
In the evening you perhaps grab
a book, I do not know what other
splendid things may happen to you.
Is a single day not exceedingly rich;
whoever uses his hours to the fullest,
whoever is not lazy, will live ten times longer
and enjoy twenty times the happiness.
If you walk through life with open arms,
you will feel at home like in a beautiful
house no matter where you go,
where everything is neat and sensible,
the old and the young see themselves
in the right light and respect each other
and thus get along, where women
are revered and men are gracious
and brave and children are well behaved.
O, it is wonderful on this earth,
be happy and grateful that you are
allowed to live here and be its citizen.

OCTOBER

Leaves are falling from the trees,
green changes into yellow,
and a delicate breeze circles the land.
October has a friendly face;
does it not resemble a genteel,
noble gentleman, does it not offer
you apples and pears and succulent
grapes and nuts? Although
the beautiful, warm nights
are gone, the days are still blue,
and there is no lack of warmth.
October reminds us of the poet
Lenau and walking. The latter
is now splendid; you walk across
a meadow and then enter the forest,
which is so bright and sunny,
it makes you happy, and quiet
and louder and clearer thoughts
pass through your soul.
Is it not something spirited, soulful,
walking around in this peaceful realm?
I have always been calm in autumn,
believed in it like a symbol of luck,
and looked up at the sky with extreme
joy and all around at life
that then seemed almost exalted.
Flowers must indeed wither,
people too grow older,
that is how it should be,
yet I think, and you may be
thinking the same,

that there exists a new bloom,
and a former bloom, which follows
you through past experiences
and never dwindles, because it
lies behind you. Despite the love
you felt, and all the good
and beautiful that gave
itself to you, your striving,
your achievements that now,
fadeless, glisten brightly
in twilight's shadows,
be glad, be gentle and kind
and patient.

AFTER DRAWINGS BY DAUMIER

A poet stands in front of a mirror,
later he shines in the salon
with his recitation of verses.

A peasant peeks into a living room.
'Bonjour, Madame,' he says, and lifts
his hat, the pretty mistress smiles.

A car goes down a dusty road,
the master is at the wheel, and his servant
sits in the back. 'Where are we going?'
They would love to know.

I'll be damned, who is that lying in the grass?
Seems like he is quite comfortable here,
otherwise he would probably be somewhere else.
In any case, it does not look like he has been
affected much by the spirit of the times.

We are in a coffeehouse.
'Pale or dark?' asks the waiter.
The customer replies, 'As you see
fit.' Is he not an odd fellow?

A man sits in a pleasure boat, when
suddenly a steamer heads toward him,
he shouts: 'Oh dear, je suis perdu.'
Many have believed themselves lost,
but luckily in the end they were not.

And the best for last: a gentleman sits

in a barbershop, when he suddenly
sees a pair of lovers go by,
he runs outside with a lathered
face, stands frozen, as if he has seen ghosts,
and says: 'What is this, c'est ma femme.'

APOLLO AND DIANA BY LUCAS CRANACH

Apollo:
What was I looking for all day,
what was it that dazzled my senses?
And now that evening has come,
here and there the sun gilds
the occasional branch,
otherwise all is still in the realm,
only a soft breeze still moves about,
and who do I meet here just now?

Diana:
I am bewildered, and justifiably so.
What did you do all day long,
not knowing your own disposition,
not sensing your own true calling,
not considering your patient, eternal
nature, and completely misunderstanding
yourself and the life that surrounds you?

Apollo:
I was hunting! Can you not tell already
by my bow and arrow that I carry?

Diana:
Of course I see it, I am scolding you.

Apollo:
I have found you, so my hunt
is glorious, and I praise it,
for I have never seen a more
beautiful, charming quarry.

But this is not the right word:
Picture—I should have said picture.

Diana:
You are too kind for such cruel
business, and I beg you,
give it up altogether now,
forget it and embrace another.
The blond curls on your head,
the lenient look in your eyes,
which are blueish like sky-light
and placid like the flood of rivers and lakes,
your benevolent gestures
and your thoughtful brow,
they all tell me that you have
a soul and are rich with talent
and are much too highly gifted
to be playing only a hunter.

Apollo:
It seems I did not even know what I was
doing and went hunting out of boredom,
it helped me pass the time, that is all.

Diana:
And that is why you kill animals?

Apollo:
Yes, that is exactly why, because I wanted to.

Diana:
You pursue poor and innocent
creatures, such as this gentle doe here,

which has with its soft body
served as my seat like it was as an armchair,
this being, which cannot speak, can only
sigh when you have wounded it,
miserably swimming in its own blood!
O, renounce such ways,
mourn for the lost time
you have wasted with your hunter's lust,
put down your bow and arrow, grab a lyre
and devote yourself to gracious art,
be protector and enthusiast
of all that is beautiful and just.

Apollo:
I love you and I cannot
but listen to you intently.
So let me say that I will let go
of the hunt and all other distractions,
and from this day on my actions
will forever be based on emotions,
and I will always first think a little
before I act, so that nobody will
have to suffer because of me, for
everything and everyone is allowed
to live, flowers and animals and people.
Everything that feels joy and pain is now
sacred to me, for I too feel both.
This is what I have just learned from
your mouth, my saviour, and it shall
not have passed its sentence in vain.
Thus from now on I will do nothing
but be affectionate.

Diana:
>   I believe you.
Go on and sing beautiful love songs.

Apollo:
You yourself are the most beautiful song.

Diana:
Then take me as your guide.

Apollo:
I would love to just stay here with you,
do nothing but look into your eyes,
your sweet smile alone would be
worth this endless pleasure.

Diana:
Good! But restrain yourself a little;
everything has its limits
and measure, but keep calm,
my friend. Go on now, it is late already,
I am sure we will see each other again soon.

THE CHRSTMAS TREE

Why should we care about the cold night?
There is such a lovely glow in the living room.
There stands a little tree on the table,
spangled with silver and gold,
hung with amusing little treats,
and candles are on the green boughs,
which flicker almost like stars now,
and now the door opens,
a throng of children hungry
for knowledge steps inside,
gently led by their parents.
They show and explain to them
the tree's glowing apparition.
Are the children not almost blissful?
That goes without saying.
Such delicate, pure, decent souls are still
capable of the most profound happiness.
And what altogether new thing comes next?
The Holy Child enters the room,
the enchantress, the gracious fairy,
white as snow and sweet as sugar
and merciful like an unearthly
being, as if she still resided
in the heavenly kingdom
and came straight from God,
and now she opens her mouth and speaks:
'Because you have all been nice and
behaved well throughout the year,
and done nothing sinful,
I have brought you all kinds
of presents.' With this she

leads them to the tree and gives
each one a present and smiles,
and the children do so as well
and thank their dear parents
for their faith and diligence,
and they kiss them, so they
can all in the best possible spirit
be happy and good to each other.
What a holy and noble celebration
and wonderfully lovely feelings,
and while they are so very glad in
their intimate circle and embody
what it means to be part of something,
bells are ringing throughout the world,
so wherever people live,
love and trust can come alive.
How bad would things be, when such
celebrations were no longer important
to us, thank God we are not there yet.—

POEMS WRITTEN IN BERNE
(1924–1933)

Can It Wish Me Anything Other than Happiness

CAN IT WISH ME ANYTHING OTHER THAN HAPPINESS

I would like to quickly write a few more poems,
to see a few objects.
Down in the garden stands a high bar,
which has a beauty mark.
Once two discordant counts lived
in the peaceful Basel region.
A barely visible narrow path
led to the laced-up relationship of both.

But nobody walked
this path.
Left to themselves,
they were forced to hate each other,
unable to contain themselves.
Whoever is no longer open to a path
has caused himself terrible sorrow,
worse than knowing death is near.
A small bird greeted
me this morning with a cheerful peal.
Let me tell you about a most peculiar case
of courtesy: an esteemed
figure with a fine reputation
amused himself by
tying my tie for me,
as if he had somehow
discovered my own clumsiness,
I put up with it and remained very calm,
I found the hand that patronized me
nice and gentle. Is it not often very
sensible to act less than bright,
to amuse others with your awkwardness?

Who would never want to act modestly?
It is better to get warm than to freeze.
You surely know the little town Büren,
it sits along a beautiful stream,
it is not quite as large as Rome,
the stream runs into the ocean.
Where is all this serenity coming from,
which soothes me,
gently empowers me?
Love,
what else could it wish for than my lasting happiness?

HOW THE SMALL HILLS SMILED

You should have seen
the little trees, their gestures
were so funny, it felt like
they were dancing, in its silver-
white cleanliness a small cloud
resembled a dolphin, you
should have seen the small hills
smiling yellow-green, it is a shame
you did not see the train
that passed by on gold-black rails,
severe and gentle, quiet
and massive, beautifully sluggish
and laborious yet marvellously light.
And I find it infinitely regrettable
that you also could not see the passengers
staring out the windows.
One like the other stared at me,
who lay in the grass,
counting timber steps
leading up the hillside,
who looked over the bridges,
and who was happy
in earth's bosom.
A factory chimney
lost itself into the heights,
a little girl walked in the distance.
I thought, seeing everything around me
in such happiness, such cheerfulness,
I ought to dissolve fairylike
and bent my head backward:
Oh, how beautiful that was!

There are so many aspirations,
but it does not take much
to have one aspiration.

THE ALLEY

She struggled against a bottomless pain,
by then we were walking down the alley,
through which an unspeakably soft breeze,
like a pleading and charming child,
trembled along and wreathed, many a time
we stood still, catching a beautiful view of the land,
which would sink deeply into our souls,
an invisible bird sang throughout
the sunset sea, the branches hung
like splendid raiment in this singing;
the velvety green grass was already a song
in itself, which resembled a pretty girl.
The constant sights and wonderment slowed
our progress and we almost despaired
of having entered such an ornate temple.

SUNDAY MORNING FLAGS

Startled lanterns sparkle
in a pale shimmer.
Into what distances
are you flying, clouds, and where else
in this sunshine are people still sitting on benches?
How lovely the flags,
as if they wanted to remind me of something,
sunlit and winding,
like children playing,
singing and happy,
and like roses, swaying
in a gentle breeze, toward the trees,
which make me dream on a Sunday
morning, sink down.

SUN

It has been a long time
since you last caressed me with your cheek,
you kept your delight
all to yourself, dear sun.
How dare you,
my little rascal,
to hide in such a rude manner,
what ought to wake me daily in a kind way.
How cowardly,
to make yourself so obscure,
so unfamiliar and lost,
instead of smiling
for people and all the colourful things.
What kind of lofty bad mood
came over you, underling?
From now on you shall be busy shining,
or I will cry,
remember that,
and love me steadily.
Never again take your golden glow
from me,
you wondrous, sweet, cheeky wench.

THE PLEASURE CASTLE

How I would treat myself there:
it would be fun no doubt.
I quickly renounced
all of my apparent dignity.

Not being dignified,
I would still carry many a burden,
I wrote in my diary,
how much I would like it there.

THE LONGED-FOR ISLAND

O, island, to long for your oak trees,
your house surrounded by vines,
the abundance of silence and the soft
nestingness of a lake,
is there anything more natural?
There cupids circle
mistresses, goats graze in the grass,
and like in days past, bells
peal, and water laps against
the cheerful piece of land.
There they hold hands
and get married, and how sweetly
you sleep there in the tidy room,
breathe crystalline air. How beautifully
all voices fade away in the high
temple of the countryside, and nights
and days are brothers,
and people get along.
O, how it sounds like peace there.

WINTER (I)

It snows, it snows, covering the many roofs and gables
with flakes that resemble the songs of Anna Siebel.

A chimney sweeper in the flurry of snow smiles softly.
Could it be that now and then he also has written a poem?

Then a garret door opens, and a little face,
which actually sparkles like a little poem,

appears to the one freezing, and a lovely, fine hand
offers him a cup with a beautifully painted rim.

The most beautiful lips whisper: 'Here, my friend, take a sip.
The warmth of this drink will tide you over.'

The chimney sweep is well-mannered and thanks her politely.
I hope, and reasonably so, that a small payment awaits me.

SPRING (II)

It blooms and sprouts, it covers the many, cute shrubs
with tiny buds; watching this, I think about Mister Deucher,

who one day expressed his favourable opinion about me,
when I felt my recruit's honour and conscience injured.

Apparently back then I was supposed to have been politely
and thoughtfully engaged in being injurious to a comrade.

The exciting altercation happened in the dining room of the
                                                    Kornhauskeller.
Today, however, I feast with great delight on this

sight of young leaves, besides a cup of chocolate,
and try my best to capture this dear spring.

O, sweetheart, when all sorts of things had to evolve this way,
now you can find flowers, which kiss you with their scent.

THE LAD IN THE CARPATHIANS

Thinking about his girlfriend,
who is working in the living room
down on even land, the lad lay,
his lithe body stretched out in the grass.
On the street, which cut through
the mountain range,
regiments were marching.
In the bluishly veiled
distance, the music of
battle, which sounded like
a dream. A song escaped
from three girls walking
on a hill, and the blooming
meadows and the forest
all seemed to join in.
An old man was walking
with the songstresses, for whom,
when they had finished singing,
in admiration for the sweetness
and comfort that had passed their
fate-exalting lips, the lad
took off his hat.

CHRISTMAS TREE

A Christmas tree, come, children, enter,
has delightful eyes, sparkling little eyes,
outside, fitting the festive season, it is snowing,
fleeting, busy, charming, ceaseless,
something singing is on the Christmas tree,
silver tinsel, swan fluff,
a small angel, fidgeting rascals are decorating
the grave little tree to bring about its delight.
Now the well-behaved boy reads poems,
in parts his problems become quite severe,
but he manages, he pulls it off,
the living room floor is strewn with glittery sand,
the young reciter smiles,
the small candlelight flickers, fans,
nuts, apples and pears
resplendent beneath luminous stars.
High on the treetop a moon sits enthroned,
on the lips of a girl lives a familiar wonderment,
everyone feels richly rewarded,
round-eyed dolls rest in armchairs.
As if it was only yesterday
when they were happy about their presents,
the grownups feel warm all over.
The jingle of sleighs sounds from the street,
a brat sits in the junk room,
which is as dark as his deed,
and the reason why he is unable
to see anything, they are singing
of dear things,
of toys, dancing shoes, rings,
may only a small part of this merry song
reach his ears,
it seems I have nearly penned a Christmas carol here!

SENSATION

What was for so long before my eyes,
what made me cheer up, and yet what
could not calm me, nature,
will very soon be far, far outside.
I will do without it and with delight
sing the praise of its brilliance, this ear-splitting
of sounds and colours. Somehow
I will miss it and so redouble my love,
as if it were still a riddle to me.
It is beautiful everywhere,
as long as we see beauty from within ourselves.
Do not listen to false insistence.
Something you enshrine will always be with you.

THE SEASONS

When you want to be popular with yourself,
you imagine all kinds of delights,
that spring is wonderful like a child
smiling from her little bed, for example,
and summer, you fancy,
is a young, capricious woman; autumn is
a talented boy adorned with the grapes
of the first spiritualization,
and alleyways of a medieval town
and streamers on a sailboat
enchanted by the cool atmosphere.
When I ask myself, what would winter be,
I am delighted for half an hour, before
I explain him to myself, by his fresh
face; thereafter I arrive with a girl
and claim that winter's holy
solitude seems virginal to me.
The seasons move almost in a circle
around my internal and external being.
In spring birds twitter,
sometimes loudly, sometimes softly.
Past the child who plays with hoops,
it goes up the steps to the golden
height of the will to live and down
to settle on the old man's staff.

THE FOREST (II)

In spring the forest resembles, I dare say,
a hesitant question, who would take the chance
not to be delighted by the forest in summer?
I once lay stretched out on a hillside:
that is how a painter painted me, and ever
since, I am known to be a dreamer. Oh, the forest
looks so very intimate in autumn, like a soul
adorned with nothing but faithfulness. New
books sometimes become new again only
after a few years have passed; this is a process
that nobody controls. How magnificently
does frost grace the forest on sunny and clear
winter days, when it all froze overnight,
as if it resembled a white-haired old man.
Thus every season
dresses the forest, given time,
he grows smart, who does not question
everything before he happily forgives a mistake.

SPRING FLOWERS

How carefully Goethe treated the German language.
In order to open myself to a modest delight,
I went on a walk, until I had the chance to see
how all the lovely flowers were strolling about.
I was quite surprised by their cheerful movements
and fleet escape, for they can normally thrive
only where they are rooted to the ground.
They are born to be smiled at and only their
keeping calm protects them from being harmed,
or so I thought, yet now it was all different,
every day you learn something new, and knowing
interruptions cannot interfere with my belief
that those flowers felt like going on a walk. Imagine it,
thus you say yes to me, and that is fine in itself,
while a no can never be a ray of sunshine for you.

HOW I SAW A LEAF FALLING

Had I not turned
around for the already
partly naked branches,
I would have missed
the sight of an intricate
summer's leaf falling
slow and golden.
I would not have seen
something beautiful and
felt something lovely, calm
and charming, soul-hardening.
Look back more often,
if you want to save yourself.
Nothing is done by looking straight ahead.
Those who never looked around did not see it all.

PARADE

Flawed elements naturally
asserted themselves again this time;
I am thinking of important behaviour,
incidentally, I am not going to rhyme
this poem, so as not to make it sound
playful, and because today I want to
turn poetry into a children's game, oh,
someone, who founded a publishing house
with a rosy future in this green land, where he
went bankrupt, I saw standing in the crowd.
A line of costumed people passed by.
Some arrived late for the show, others stood
there already before there was anything to see;
to me an Amazon seemed the most beautiful,
sitting on her horse, as if hordes of believers
had, after a journey of longing, arrived
at a beautiful and secret destination.
You will understand when I say that I
might have found a monster interesting
for the sake of its fang-pointed advice.
But it was all play, and the demons
were already thinking about their
double-litres later at a cosy place.
A girl in the garb of a peasant
pretended to cry; beautiful seemed
the wagon that brought to mind
a wedding, and a house, knocked
together by the builders' songs
zigzagging into the sky, floated by.
The cook threatened gracefully
with her ladle, and out of colourful

centuries a scribe was radiant
with the poise of an inkwell.
A flag thrower who like a dancer
let the country flag climb into the air;
it fell always, like a possession,
back into his hand; it seems every
skill deserves a quick applause.

CHRISTMAS

I once read in a book
about a town as fragile as glass;
the roofs, towers, gables
had something of a brooch about them,
and such very pretty things were there,
prettier ones have never been seen.
Every year around Christmas
actors came into the hamlet
with heroines and novices
and brand-new jokes.
How awesome was Amelia's dispatching
of Franz Moor in the park.
Delightfully she drew the dagger
for herself and her beloved.
Hamlet, the Dane, marched
tragically onstage, and Othello,
the giant, fell to the ground
with jealous gestures.
Back when you were still a boy,
you acted out tales of Karl May
in the woods, and let me herewith
literally recall 'Caravan of Slaves'.
During the merry Christmas season, no part
of this townscape did not resemble a dream.

THE CARROUSEL

The carrousel with all its finery
will never ever make me bitter;
looking at it, my heavy heart
quickly grows light again.
When my heart has shut itself away,
it opens up again like a door.
You look at it as if it were a kingdom,
where everything is carefully
balanced and perfectly bent.
The carrousel knows how to lie
with its pretty face, to politely
deceive you with its lovely lines,
you happily acknowledge it
and are utterly spell-bound
by its artifice, which is based on
cunning, which has always been
the case with things that make us
happy and cheerful. It spins around,
and this makes you a bit dim,
yet that is exactly why it is clever:
while I watch it spinning around,
I believe it carries me away,
but belief is always your weak side,
it is mostly nothing but adornment.
The carrousel speaks: 'I am here
pretending to be spinning in place
as both distance and nearness.'

SUNDAY WALK

During my Sunday walk, which I quietly took yesterday,
it is a given that my cheerfulness made me laugh softly.

Like every Sunday, a few people were smoking their pipes,
on the head of a little girl a ribbon fluttered in the air.

The scenery watched me like a theatre crowd.
How taken I am by this spectacle of nature,

as if my years still made me a youth,
as if I had just now reached adult age.

Romanesque a steeple stood in God's pretty
acre, whereupon I bravely took a look around

the quaint, solemn sanctuary of the church,
and time passed in quite a natural way.

When you have, as they say, bummed around enough,
you will spontaneously walk back to the city.

IN THE HOSPITAL

Until the lovely little flowers
would show me their fair eyes of wonder,
I decided to practice on the fiddles
of effortless patience,
the mountains shimmered over there.
Yes, when I lay sick in bed,
I longed for a lively day,
for people, friends and acquaintances,
I chatted to the nameless
and always only imagined the seconds,
and the hours seemed wonderfully round.
Oh, in the hospital
I enjoyed infinite tenderness.

AUTUMN (I)

Autumn arrives quietly,
as if it did not care
when it arrives, when it leaves
and where it begins and ends.

Here and there a leaf falls already,
which does not struggle in its fall.
The descent from a tree
resembles childish prattle.

The child has brown eyes,
whom I dedicate these lines to,
which I gently set down here,
while I am rubbing my eyes.

For in autumn it is proper,
because summer is gone,
to pretend you are crying
a melancholy tear.

SNOW (III)

Tonight, the entire city
is a fairy-tale-like white splendour.
I gingerly walked outside
in the snow, busy falling
snow, to rejoice
in a loud voice.
Although I just lie from here on out;
it does not befit such a fine gentleman, as I
would like to be, to scream his lust for life.
This is what the rude ones bring along,
who do not submit to more tender bidding.
I then really walked very quietly
through the non-existent moonlight,
because it was snowing. Snow is not hard,
rather it is soft, wet and delicate;
falling snowflakes
are more flattering than dry.
It is as if they kissed
you, as if they knew,
as if the gentle, fresh snow knew
that it will not hurt the little nose or cheek
it touches with its fluff.
Unless I am gravely mistaken,
my dogged being a stay-at-home allowed me
to coax out a valuable winter scene.

A SHORT LETTER

Oh, charming,
I tell you,
is early snowfall
in the dawning open air.
School children are going to school,
when the sun has yet to shine.
When morning steps
out of night,
it is still dark,
but its cheeks,
as soon as it strikes eight or nine,
catch fire.
Oh, how dear,
how good existence can be.
You should knock there
whenever it pleases you.

LONGING

The meat, the beer, the bread
one consumes every day,
how shall I say this quickly?
You, my ever-pervading longing,
like the rush of rivers, the widening of plains,
that is how it appears to me, and women
exist who dare to write how
they were once good to me
for a pleasant evening, their letters
breathe a measured coolness from this depth
of thought and feeling they forgot—
and, perhaps now sitting at a sewing table,
remembering after many years
how they were moved by something,
they play thoughtfully with their hair.
My longing, and the longing of everyone else
wander, colourfully tangled.

SPRING

Who would like to desecrate spring
by writing a bunch of poems?
Children are practicing ring-around-a-rosy,
you can hear the cuckoo calling like a cuckoo
and spring-delighted boys and girls yelling, Hurray!
As if it were about to snow all kinds of delicacies,
small flowers grow in rows of two and three
everywhere, to make their charming likeness,
to lend words to the marvellous,
the poetling walks in the fresh air.

WINTER (II)

In order that summer does not remain,
wearing a fur coat, winter now
arrived on a horse-drawn sleigh.
As is well known, trees bloom in May.

Now, however, they stand there leafless,
and lakes and rivers are frozen,
you can see fingertips and ears
already glowing from the cold.

The ice skates are strapped on,
the frozen surface quickens with figures,
having fun knows no boundaries,
even if the sport is a hundred years old.

The winter cold gives me
reason to stretch my legs.
Whatever is important to me
will thus love me a little too.

CHRISTMAS BELLS

When it snows, because it is winter,
you like to form a family circle at home,
where you play music with graceful eagerness.
When the season sheds its warmth,
even though it is nice that flakes are falling,
you will gladly allow a dear book to guide you,
while reading you can think of anything,
and embraced now by your memories,
you have entered into the spirit of youth.
When you go outside, you find the temperature
pleasant, and you can walk through the streets
almost as if through neatly cleaned rooms,
and a fiery red and bashful cheek perhaps
in spirit accompanies you on this walk
through your city, snowflakes
rhyme happily to the bells.
This could be the sound of Christmas bells,
and candlelight and a sip of wine,
and a small modest gift.

SNOW (IV)

The woods seem asleep now,
similar to the lambs and sheep.
I too am covered with snow,
as if I were hiding from myself.
Snow lies happily on all the roofs,
like long forgotten letters in boxes,
and it is dark in the drawers,
and there is a sparkling of notes
at the concert, and in the halls
candles flash, and now and then
a good joke causes bright laughter.
Snow is magnificent!
The scenery looks like
a bed made for a child,
and poets are busy writing poems.
Machines hiss on the floors,
where there is no time to dally.
Young lads, girls, women and men,
what hopes do you have?
Snow now lies on all the roads.
What a beautiful time it is!
In the field, blades of grass
cut through the snow.
Wherever it lands, it settles,
does not move, and will not budge.

IN THE FOREST

Like iron bars on a gate,
the fir trees tower up.
What can you see in this forest,
except that slender trees stand?

The day vanishes, night comes soon.
Before it grows dark in the forest,
I proceed through the fir trees
and later walk away in silence.

Sometimes I would love to know
where my life star is guiding me,
but it is nice to dream pleasantly
among these slender trees.

THE JOYS OF BATHING

O, how I long for the land
where water's frills splash
against the rocky and flowery edges;
in the past I often found happiness there.

My pale or tanned feminine hand
would be blissful on that tempting beach,
where the houses see themselves as a haze
in the smooth mirror, where winds blow
and trees stand, whose leaves tremble
just for fun, where whispering
tales roam the pretty scenery,
where you believe rapturously, even
though you are unable to hear a sound.

There I was rocking in a small boat,
rather than playing notes on my piano
in a room with papered walls.
How I long for the unspoiled sand
on the shore, to gently caress the waves
as I bathe freely in this vast space.

TRAVELLING

How lovely it is to travel,
you get on a train,
you are dressed comfortably,
houses and trees fly by,
as if they were delicate dreams.
The wheels rattle softly.
Somehow you strike up
a conversation with someone
and already you are almost friends,
travelling has a certain timbre to it,
consisting of friendliness and heedlessness,
and a trace of respect for life,
not too little and not too much.
Of course you decide on a destination,
but you do not really care about it.
What is important becomes trivial,
because it is just a game to you.
Today you are here and tomorrow there,
who travels goes from place to place,
the cities, towns, rivers, lakes,
the alleyways, schoolbags, girls, boys,
the station halls, reading rooms,
and anything else you saw
you later write down in your notebook,
for it remained in your memory.

EVENING (III)

Evening, how vast you are
compared to the leaping
smallness of morning,
which lacks feelings.
To have it in your heart
is so wonderfully strange.
Its cheek is flushed
due to the sun's farewell.
Must it be embarrassed
for being so soulful?

CIRCE

How nice it must be to sit in a bark
and go on your nightly excursion.
The lake lies spread out like a silk coat
and has gently beckoned me to come to it.
The surface of the water glistens darkly bright,
how solemn is heedlessness and slowness quick.
The moon hangs down from above like a lamp in a room,
life resembles a stage; with gestures as delicate as
birch twigs, Circe appears centre stage,
she who brings to mind misfortune and happiness.

THE ISLAND

There, beneath ancient oak trees, still
stands a dance hall from years past.
Even today on occasion couples
spin around until they get tired or
the flutes and violins take a break.
O, how happy the leaves are that they
are allowed to thrive on this island.
Waves ripple and dance around the
soon high and soon low shore, and in
a building that used to be a cloister,
people are eating like it was a tavern,
and old and neatly cut rocks, which you
can find in the wonderful forest,
point to a formerly hardworking people.
The island itself seems to breathe merrily,
to take pleasure in its feminine existence.

SWITZERLAND

On the hills of the midlands
there stand tall linden trees;
cities politely nestle against
the shores of beautiful lakes.
Across the Jura lay narrow
and broad heights. Compared
with the snow-white fairies,
there are on the other hand
massive mountains we call the Alps,
they are known far and wide,
their icy defiance is their charm,
for they will not relinquish their place.

A GLASS OF BEER

In this grove's adornments,
I think of a glass of beer,
then I quietly walk on
as if on a narrow stepladder.
Pretty young girls pass
amicably through the thicket,
now and then I stand still,
because I want it to suit me.
I have overcome the glass of beer,
which could have tasted so good.

THE TINY VILLAGE

I sit on a bench
and gratefully look
with fresh and open eyes
into the distance for a while.

Alluringly a breeze
moves through the
forest, like an invisible,
cheerful, dear child.

I send my warmest regards
to the sweet and gentle
tiny village I see before me,
it looks like it is nodding.

Time passes happily,
I am at ease here and dream,
as if I were a kind of scene,
like a village, wind and tree.

AUTUMN (II)

In autumn we think of artists and poets
who dedicate their existence to the beautiful.
The trees ablaze with yellow leaves
resemble a wallpapered chamber,
wherein a lady flirts with her page.
This short season's inherent
golden eyes are enchanting,
like a lover's bliss
or the illusion of a girl.
Why are we so full of dreams in autumn?
Because there is an ineffable need
in whomever is part of life
and delights in apples and grapes
to give rest to all greed?
Oh, how many mistakes does man commit,
and is not this exactly the reason why he loves
autumn's face with its knowing smile?

THE LITTLE TOWN

Sleeping houses look like they
are nodding to each other.
The town hall and the post office
sway to and fro with proud joy.
Those who want to enter the church
will find it beautiful and lovely and silent.
The tavern, the publishing house
happily go about their business.
An ancient castle stands on the height,
fleas dance in the sunshine,
you can also call them gnats.
In this pretty town you think
about stories from years past,
about aunts, uncles, cousins, nieces,
and how nice it is to write poems here.
A stream gallantly runs by,
as if it were a silk ribbon.
Busy workshops confidently
stare out across the region,
kind women sit at the windows,
who are seeking something worth seeing.
A car stops in front of a house,
a newcomer cheekily jumps out,
and dog, cat, sparrow, girl
also play a part in this image of a town.

VACATION

How nice it was for the children
to get out into the countryside,
not to see for a while the streets
and people, but to be able to
climb trees. In the country
house the family stayed at
to spend a happy vacation,
there were lots of neat rooms.
To roll down the hill in a
wooden cart, to explore
the countryside without shoes
or socks was lovely. In the evenings
you could sit on the terrace and catch
a glimpse of the city, which always gives
you much to talk about, and which, once
the vacation is over, you will gladly see again.

EVENING (IV)

In the evening the trees stand still like a dream,
as if someone was trying to think of something,
there is not even the hint of a breeze, and there
is seemingly no branch willing to be in motion still.

THE READER

With one of those train station dime store books,
he settled into his nest.
He saw how the hotel governesses banished
him with their disapproving stares.
The nest I have just mentioned
bribed him with its privacy,
it was a fine spot shaded
by delicate twigs, above him
and his book, his dreaming, the putti
dip down to his head with caresses,
flies are buzzing amid lush leaves
and turn toward the fragrant scent,
and he who is reading the little book,
happy with its interesting content,
surrounded by flowers soft and kind,
wastes precious time without a care.

THE CHURCH

How pleasant it was in that small church,
where the thought of community
allowed souls to come alive. A girl
struck me with her gushing praise,
and a woman, whom I thought I knew,
with her almost overly severe character,
perhaps she was afraid of her heart's desires,
because to feel is not proper. The eloquent
pastor's mouth spoke words of hope
and patience. Every now and then
a person running late entered the interior
of the house of God, which glorified
peacefulness. When Mass was over
and you stepped outside, the small crowd
of people was delighted to see the starry night,
and then scattered in all directions.

THE LITTLE ONES

They got something to read,
because they were well-
behaved in days past,
the cute, little persons.

Things to play with and laugh
are surely more than fitting
when it comes to bringing joy
to the tender hearts of children.

To receive presents
is not very difficult.
Sweet are the treasures
hanging on the Christmas tree.

There is pleasure taken in gifts
for those gifted with a fine
sense of discretion and children
with the joyous faith they have.

JOY OF LIFE

How beautiful it is when you are silent,
when you stop talking to yourself.
There you see happy and beautiful
people, charmingly joined into a circle,
enjoying their conversations beneath
the trees, tiny dancers who move
to the rhythm of a concert. Nature
is a sugar baker's confection; costumes,
elegant gestures! On the water
those who rock in boats delight
in their gliding over a mirror,
the landscape seems painted,
life, you imagine, is eternal,
and an unpleasant parting from these
gracious, flowered pastures, impossible.
How difficult it is to dress this dying
and its harsh suffering in fertile words.

INVITATION

Come and see me some time,
it will be worth the effort,
on the heights and in the vale
cows graze without a thought.

Do not bother with ideas,
when no thoughts at all
quarrel inside your head,
everyone will be glad to see you.

Cheer up and come,
I will give you a nice welcome,
the pious birds will sing,
once you wish to be here.

The flowers and the grass,
the delicate leaves,
this I assure you,
happily expect your footsteps.

APRIL

Faces are red and blue,
the weather behaved like Ringelnatz,
the rowdy wind ran around
carelessly and not calm at all,
did not care to be friendly.

I too ran as fast as the wind,
I love to brawl with it,
to be lively like April
in rain and in sunshine,
and to take a breather afterward.

SUMMER

In summer we eat green beans,
peaches, cherries and melons.
In every sense nice and long,
the days make a sound.

Trains travel through the country,
flags flap merrily on rooftops.
How nice it is in a boat
surrounded by gradual heights.

The high peaks still wear snow,
flowers give fragrance. On the lake
you can spend all your time
singing and being happy.

I do not know what it is that makes me rich,
you lie in the grass and read a book
and from everywhere you hear
the pointless gnats, buzzing flies.

BOAT RIDE

The ride on the water was
lovely and gentle in every sense.
On the shore stood slender cedar trees,
feathers fell from women's bonnets.
The boat floated on and on;
we all happily put up with
possibilities and boundaries.
Time passed with pleasantry
and flattery; the day was long.
With the sound of a mandolin
you landed on a pretty spot
where you could sit in the grass.
The many thousand leaves
seemed to enjoy themselves.
The food tasted good in the open air,
as if it were roasted pigeons.
In the evening you withdrew from
this happiness back to your home.
Many would savour the memories
of hours spent in such a wonderful way.

IN THE WOODS

How it always feels like home,
when I stand in the forest,
which I have done many a time,
and see but beauty around me.

Unless I am gravely mistaken,
I then meander here and there
and feel like I am in a room,
shrouded in a painted glow.

It wants to show me all of its
kind and friendly things,
and never, unless I am open to it,
has it caused me any boredom.

I happily decided to waste
my time here and dream,
with all the countless leaves,
amongst its scented trees.

WINTER (III)

Everything is so nice and quiet,
you think you are still in bed.
Winter wants me to see its beauty
with all the snow everywhere.

Painters paint magical pictures.
Do I not feel myself growing
calm in the gradual realization
that I have lost so many things?

It is apparently quite smart
and good to hibernate.
To look across the white meadow
offers you peace and faith.

Snow is as nice as forgiveness,
which wants to thrive by itself.
Look at how it lies on lanes and hedges,
and to think we had nothing to do with it!

THE TRAVELLING JOURNEYMAN

The half-moon is still visible,
the early day is still dark.
There is nothing to fix in this scenery,
nothing one would want to correct.

Greeting lovely nature,
he takes leave of the lodging house.
Sweetening his soul with courage,
he now continues on his life's path.

The birds trill thoroughly bird-like,
the fir trees stand slender and silent,
while walking he will perhaps turn
once more to look at the building.

'Hey, Journeyman, why so chipper?'
'I don't know,' he answers . . .
'You'll get off it soon enough!'
'Then I'll just get up again.'

The nice building is gone now,
but to this day you can still spot
a journeyman's manner and ways
as he cheerfully begins another journey.

SLEEP WELL

Sleep well with your cute,
innocent and funny dimples,
rest sweetly on your pleasant moods
in this small and fragrant house.

Sleep well, my lovely sweetheart.
Does my poem not resemble a thief
who sneaks into your hearkening ears,
while your pretty mouth tells me to hush?

The Child Ponders

THE CHILD PONDERS

Often well-to-do people have deceived us
by pretending to be poorer than the poor.
What I did and did not have was also both visible and hidden.
Do strong men not occasionally resemble weak boys,
when they gloat over the weakness of others?
Ravens lie in wait over the pastures of our lack of judgement.
'Mistress, be as critical of yourself as you are of the riff-raff,'
I call out to her confidently as her devout child.
Honeycombs
are delicious meals.
Slowly and quickly,
I will surely find my way to her once more.

DAILY ROUTINES

People learned how to be moderate,
and that is why they called them mediocre.
At noon they went to eat lunch,
happily performed their tasks,
in order to enjoy their nightly sleep
in nice beds and to experience
the same orderly process the next
day, and with a brazen nimbleness
the trains jumped onto their rails,
which gleamed bluish in the sunshine,
into the distance, to turn up at this or that
spot according to the railway schedule.
Girls and boys loved each other mechanically,
and husband and wife tried to compose themselves;
children skipped obediently to school,
and each year banks announced
their formidable net profit.
In order not to recklessly catch fire,
I too controlled my temper more and more.

THE FURNISHED ROOM

When you put too much into it,
a space will only grow smaller.
It can easily become overgrown
with furniture and pictures.
Sofa, bed, chair and closet
will sicken its narrowness, so to speak.
Many other things
in the room are laughable.
The tiny jars, the figurines and shells
seem to talk and whisper.
The covers, pillows, tassels
will not be very agreeable
with the idea of the contemporary.
Bygone things too subtly knick-knack
at the workmanship of the day; a space grows
larger, brighter, more reasonable, smarter,
when you do not cover its former face
by cramming it full with decorations
to make it seem like something else,
something richer and more luxurious.
The room in and of itself gives the room
enough character and lustre.
A lot of people would do splendidly well
without doing and knowing too much.
You would be much more
if you did not weigh yourself down
so much with who knows
what kind of rubbish.
The constant keeping and collecting
will give you wrinkles
and make you look old and icy.
One's space is never there to stay
as it has been seen all along.

THE COMFORT OF COMPLAINING

No one should feel abandoned,
yet I think there are many who
imagine themselves to be alone.
Here I live like a child enchanted
by the idea that I have been forgotten.
Perhaps there are only a few of us who can
bounce back in this way. Everywhere, I say,
there is some sun and wind and shadows
and sparkling moments of happiness
and sorrow swooping down on the soul
like an eagle from the heights of humanity.
Of course, people forget each other
quickly, but I believe everyone
is to blame for the fact
that those who were forgotten
were forgetful themselves.
To complain about something so natural
has a certain comfort sometimes.

NO ONE IS FLAWED

One went here and the other
went there, and they hang,
fidget like leaves on a branch. Strange
how no one is happy anymore.
They all despair and say so openly,
as if it has been taken for granted
to no longer be sure of oneself.
The eyes watch and the ears listen
as usual, but the talent, the hope,
which is called genius, has been lost,
inside all of us lurks a kind of sorrow,
the lightness within us has become lifeless,
the difficult has become even more difficult.
It was different once. Today nobody is as
inconsolable as the happy ones used to be,
who worked hard to turn misfortune into fortune,
they fidget, tremble like leaves,
prisoners of their own indifference,
idly hanging on the branches.
No one has a single flaw anymore.
It is the flaws the flawless are missing.

THE BENEFITS OF TALKING

Whatever we can talk about to one other,
our watchful eyes have seen it already.
Talking tries hard to be good for something,
and that talk replaces a world for us.

SLEEP

But how insignificant is this life,
it seems like a friendly face
without much that is interesting.
Music is being played somewhere
in a garden, we take a stroll, eat
and drink and walk and sleep,
and everyone who claims to be
a member of society is used to
restaurants, jobs and other business.
That which we see as movement
and so on resembles sleep. Do we
all forget each other, one after another,
in life's strange bright hall?

WHY NOT BE STILL?

Why oh why do you hurry,
instead of taking your time.
How can you keep running
like that, busy making deliveries,
instead of hanging on to it
and wait and laugh,
or to sing a little song.
How can you be so swift
with your willing and docile,
overhasty little gifts,
instead of never being winded.
It is no mean feat
to buy yourself influence,
even with a spark of hard work,
you cannot make an impact.

FAMILY LIFE

You often ate dinner now and then,
cooked, ironed and stitched,
a light breeze blew through the window,
you sat still with a book for days on end.
You made and received many visits,
in the forest you saw a beech tree and
enjoyed plenty of music in the concert hall.
While the children grew older, the ones
who begot them began to slowly fade,
but the daily chores were still taken care of,
now and then the eyes saw something nice.
Linens, shoes and clothes were swapped
and fought over and knowledge questioned,
and schoolhouse, theatre and savings banks,
spoons and forks, plates, pots and cups,
taking turns saying hello and hating each other,
all put in an appearance with family life.

THE BEAUTY

Then they all just thought about their stomachs,
I mean, of delicacies prepared in the kitchen,
of the perfection of outward
appearances, of such and such
impeccable impression they would make,
clothes and house and happy smiles,
but the hearts moved ever
farther away; courage was frowned upon,
they were all very satisfied with themselves,
because they acted so reasonably, knew
how to properly deal with what is necessary,
yet they very much yearned for this feeling,
this feeling that was no longer fashionable,
from where would this beauty wing?

HIGH ART

No one will fail to attend
the waiting, the disappointment.
No matter how he marries to his advantage,
he will dig himself into a hole.
The best way to sit on the chairs
of the theatre is with a cool,
elegant, delicate, intelligent aversion,
and when the show is over,
you return home with a decent
frustration. Nobody is smart,
unless, like Verdi, they come
along at eighty with a new piece.
Nowadays everyone has debts,
and no one comes out short on forbearance.

THE BROOK

There babbles a brook
that just wants to be on its own.
Trees with their branches
dip down to the ripples
that only want to flow,
happily jump over one another.

A poet sits by lamplight
and scribbles a short poem,
life forms a circle dance,
some are talking, others are silent.
What he shall not accomplish,
he gives and takes in abundance.

DANIEL IN THE LION'S DEN

Perhaps it was because their stomachs
were full and they were lying on their prey,
that it did not occur to them. Oh, he looked
at them in such a way that they were terrified
of him, as if they had felt the awful goodness
that radiated from him like a flaming bloom.
At the edge of the lion's pit, it smelled
and rejoiced and sounded and reeked
like the victory of a godly criminal,
the perfume reached the nostrils of those
that wanted to bring about his downfall,
yet astonished shall now witness
how his gracious lights of life brought
his shaggy judges to their knees.
What do they smell on Daniel?
A meagreness of flesh and a vast soul?

YOUNG JOHN

A waterfall in the background,
a boy with a sweet mouth tells
the world about peacefulness.
With a calm hand he strokes
his little sheep, and a white ribbon
hangs down as a meaningful bauble
from the shepherd's pious crook.
The boy behaves in a very fine manner,
you can tell he is already experienced.
The slit
opens on his noble bearing,
the lovely folds of his robe.

THE CHRIST CHILD

There was not much to boast
about back then, a calf mooed
peacefully, a little donkey stood
by the manger, sniffing at the small
truss of straw with its lips,
there was no Bernard Shaw yet,
a sentence, with which I illustrate
the naivety of my dear animals,
which you saw grazing by the hillside.
As if night were nearing day,
it was bright all around,
and compared to this song here
I would like to set in motion,
the Virgin Mary kept still,
as if she were blessed; her husband
stood in the by no means splendid
hall, as if nothing serious
had ever happened here
that would bear down on him.
The shepherds would greet him now,
the one sitting childlike on her lap,
and I do not want to say anything else,
for what I am chronicling here
belongs to the history of the world.
In the narrow stable the course
of something powerful began.

MARY IN THE TENT

She only put her child on her lap
and became venerable and great.
In all imaginably beautiful ways
the kings knelt before her.
She did not know how she got it,
her husband had a pure soul.
Thus you too should have done it,
to behold with such graceful
eyes that which appeared to you,
with such majestic pudency,
with such appreciation that your love
for the child remained untouchable.
With the gifts lying at her feet,
she regards the sweet child,
and all around the roundness
of the earth a cheerfully forced
recognition makes itself known,
greetings passed from mouth to mouth.
And we have grown so smart,
to this day we still kneel before this child.
Why does the entire
world stand on
its toes before this tent,
pushing each other closer,
so they can see it?

JESUS, THE INSCRUTABLE ONE

Does he know whether he can save them?
He looks at them in such an enigmatic way,
and could it be that he is a warlock?
The girl lies so softly in her bed
and is so helpless and gaunt,
and he, the silent one, the mighty inquirer,
is he really thinking about
appearing like a giver of life now?
We see him visibly at rest within himself.
There is a chalk-
coloured suffering,
and yet his silky-soft mercy
is allowed to dress him so splendidly?
He was certainly a benevolent one,
he sacrificed himself for us,
and we will never make sense of him.

THE PERFECT ONE

He ate of the bread and drank of the wine
and then he joined in the conversation:
'One of you will certainly betray me.'
Oh, how the disciples were appalled
when such syllables reached their ears.
He sat there like one already betrayed,
for his heart saw it so clearly, as if it
had already happened, that it must happen.
He probably also heard his followers pleading:
'Admit it, such a thing is impossible,
because you are our star and guide.'
Was it his social skill and guile
to be deliberately handed over?
He was no longer in need of the applause
he always got unsolicited in the past
when he strode through the flood with a staff.
They insisted; and he said: 'Have I revealed
to you what I should not have revealed at all?'
and ate of the bread and drank of the wine.

THE SUFFERING FACE

They put you into their soup,
used you as their puppet.
You felt how they played with you,
appealed to your good intentions.
What does your face reflect now?
Why do you close your eyes?
The birds sing their songs,
soon the lilacs will bloom.
You great, kind, good man,
who can make the sick smile:
Where and when did your
beautiful thoughts begin
to wither and despair?
You no longer speak
with the power of love
you once had,
now it is but sorrow.
I long stood before you recently,
to see myself satisfied in your song.

THE CRUCIFIED ONE

Here hang the whip and birch
they used to beat him with
for the love and goodness he gave,
to make him face his own pain.
He received such hard punishment,
because his piety resembled a sheep.
Oh, my dear baby Jesus,
sadly you let go of your halo,
which is the only reason you
pitifully went to the dogs.
The wound given to you
at some point by a rude hand
resembles a mouth.
Now and then you should have
happily read some rubbish
and then softly laughed at people.
Typically, what comes from a diaper
is nothing but scum.
If you could have only let yourself be fanned by your taste,
                                        your education,

lying on rising pillows,
not torn to shreds by the whip,
just like you are depicted in museums.

WE SEE HIM SMILE

How this young woman looked
on me kindly, and loved and admired
by races that have long perished,
he continues to flow past with the same
serenity, and you still love him
to this day, even today you find him
good and great and beautiful, and he
will stay this way, but he will never know,
and he will look to us as though he were fleeing.
He leaves us unabandoned,
but it dwells in his strong nature,
and fate wants it this way,
that he is both the wanderer
and the homebody; as often as he leaves,
he returns; nobody can be as young
as him. He does not watch out for anything,
but that is exactly what is beautiful about him.
There will never come a moment when he
will see himself for what he is.
How lovely she looked at me, this young woman,
and in no way did I seem to be yearning,
and he, he, why was he invented?
So everyone can use him for all sorts of things?
When you see him so gentle, how could you think
of his thunderous fall from the cliffs!
He smiles at us, but this smile,
oh, from what wilderness has it come.—
Could it be some inclination, to be a river?

THE LOST SON

He smoked, drank and played cards
in the widely branched garden of life.
As an utter tatterdemalion,
as a downright ruin,
he stepped before his father's pious face
and said to him: 'I am lost.'
Maids and servants pricked up their ears,
the kind-hearted old man
began to sob uncontrollably
when he saw the good-for-nothing who had
returned home fall to the ground like a rag.
Rembrandt painted this moving
scene wonderfully, I believe.
Many a lovely and pretty tear has leaked
from this and that eye in the circle of visitors.
'Now I am no good for absolutely anything,'
the completely dishevelled one almost muttered
as the kind one shining brightly in the light
of love picked him up off the ground,
so that he may be upright again.
The other one, who had stayed at home,
who always fulfilled his role to a hair,
did not feel welcome in the crowd
of those, who, due to their lost son having
returned home again, heard Christmas
carols inside their bodies; he would like to be
less ill-humoured, less moody, less serious.
He had always done the right thing.
And now? Now the bad one stood
blissfully among his kind.
How can a measured mind,

in which jealousy struggles miserably,
join the newly born,
this something that has made everyone cry with joy?

DON JUAN

One day he saw a poor man
begging for pity.
With warm and poignant
words, a lady wonderfully
accused the good man.
Shoes had high heels,
girls wore colourful frocks.
He who is susceptible to attraction
resorts to trickery and cunning.
There has never been a finer
villain; an officer,
humourless, grim and stern,
gave him a warning
that he, dashing and glib,
laughed off unperturbed.
Happy and peaceful was his desire,
he was dissolute and kind.
His qualities had
sunshine as well as shade;
you struggled in vain against
the beauty of his character.
You saw him drinking, dissembling,
days and nights flew by,
with a flippant lip he laughed
about the holy principle.
Do not follow in his wake,
my esteemed colleagues!

THE PETIT BOURGEOIS

All you have to do is praise him a little,
right away he will feel unbelievably aloft;
how dependent he is,
how his petty cunning fails him;
he is just as shrewd
as he is backward;
if you dare to love him,
he will honour you with a beating;
I for one would never laud
him without trembling,
there is absolutely nothing
noble about his character;
he has no tact,
he has nothing but profit
in his eyes and cannot see
how life passes him by,
how day after day flees,
how the earth goes on without him;
the petit bourgeois never thanks his Maker,
for there is no poetry in him.

RIZZIO THE SINGER

When I attentively called on him,
he received a pretty monthly income.
The letters he wrote in a noble tone
were mostly in no need of revision.

I now report with measured haste:
Of course, he enjoyed his lovely patronage.
This son of cypresses and orange trees
was tailor-made for Love's arrows.

You cannot be superior all the time.
It was impossible for him to keep rising,
his wretchedness had to be apparent.

Spirit and talent, velvet and pomp and violins
and sweet pastime in candlelight
one day ceased to glow.

PASCIN

In essence he drew rather strange things,
a bit graceful and a little plump, I mean,
everything was fine while brazen
that flowed from his pen. At one time
I had a painting of his that my maid
despised. She asked me to remove it
from her sight. One night in the glow
of a coffeehouse concert hall on
Potsdamer Street, I met this personage,
and we whispered in conversation.
Workers were still struggling outside at this
late hour as we were walking home. The critics
sometimes delivered a blow to his prints,
in which he combined the indecent
with the decent. Lucas Cranach painted
divinely naïve nudes of an exalted naturalness,
and it will always be he who takes risks,
who is the one who was once hesitant
and then perhaps gave it up—everyone
follows his character flaws like a little dog.

VAN GOGH

The poor man
just does not do anything for me.
From his coarse palette
every pleasant view of life
scatters within me. Alas, how
bleakly painted is his life's work!
He painted, it seems to me, only well enough.
If someone wants to appear somewhat
critical at an exhibition, he would be
concerned by such brushstrokes.
Terrible how these fields, meadows, trees
interrupt one's sleep at night,
they are like clumsy dreams.
But respect is due to any fervent
artistic efforts, for example,
that painting in which you can see
the insane in the madhouse.
There is no doubt that he rendered
the blazing sun, air, earth, wind splendidly.
Yet, facing such self-tormenting work,
you do eventually lower your eyelids,
for it is but partly satisfactory work.
One is horror-stricken when art
is incapable of something more beautiful,
when it heedlessly unfurls its Must, Shall
and Will before spectating souls.
When I see a painting, my one wish is this,
to be fondled as though by some good fairy,
go, go, adieu!

THE BERNESE PAINTER ALBERT ANKER

He painted girls and boys,
public, school and farm rooms,
and when he walked through the Seeland,
he held it near and dear to his heart,
and he industriously depicted
impressive gentlemen authors,
a bride, a groom and old women,
for which he will forever be known,
and he drew grandfathers, houses, children
as decorously as they do in Paris.
One painting of his I will never forget,
it leads you into a quiet room,
where a girl who has left
this life is lying in her bed.
Because his images succeeded
in reaching something more profound,
he continued to live his life's work
with undiminished enthusiasm,
and he prevailed in his people,
for when it comes to his realism,
he shines even more than some of the new.

LINDBERGH

Oh, how the chestnut candles bloom
lovely now in the gardens of administrations.
If it were only worth it,
I would undertake a journey on foot.
But is it really necessary to always experience
and write something? When I was busy
joking around with her, with a heavy heart
my mother told me about her suffering.
Since in some sense I am
considered something of an authority,
new magazine numbers come flying in gratis.
Besides the fact that it is nice
when maids shine one's shoes black,
North America's son, who had already
achieved such great things at the age
of twenty-five, made me very ambitious
with enthusiasm
over his dashingness,
madly, so to speak, to begin with,
and no one shall come to me with art and so forth!

THE JAILHOUSE SONNET

Here, where nobly considered gestures
counted and cultivated locutions
called on submissively awaiting enquirers,
where many a heart quivered under silk waistcoats

in the course of stately and splendid parties,
and ladies and gentlemen deported themselves
discreetly, tactfully through the garden,
the land's most eminent and finest

society appeared with their graces
and airs, and where the bolts on the doors
glittered imposingly, and carriages

drawn by four horses dashed past the people,
here such as they see themselves locked up now,
who are such that they remain unmoved by them.

RIDDLES

How guilty a raffish slacker seems to the teacher.
Have you ever seen how trees move like dancers tied together?

Their immobility is an enchanted motion.
Houses are a walking, seeing, leaping fixedness.

It is like the beauty of jilted women,
the effect of productive indolence, faith's trembling mistrust.

Ruins can live, things erected can be dead,
E. T. A. Hoffmann believes a Mozart opera goes well with red wine.

It is quite easy to grow spiritually and intellectually
when your joy goes along with the joys of others.

As soon as he sees your wilfully happy face,
even the most light-hearted laughter will quit his laughter.

In the end, the disdainful desire the same as you,
and life's door will inevitably have slammed on them.

SNOW

Snow does not fall up,
but takes its course
downward and settles here,
it has never risen.

It is in every way
quiet in its being,
not a hint of loudness.
If only you were like it.

Waiting and stillness
are its most delicate,
distinctive qualities,
it lives in its being prostrate.

It never returns
to where it fell from,
does not move, has no ambition,
silence is its happiness.

CITY IN THE SNOW

It snowed into the land of evening.
As I am already on the move,
I continue to walk through the streets
and watch the glittering silver snow fall.
Some handsomely walk in pairs
and are perhaps already used to this beauty,
goodness, they have sought and found each other,
and one does not want to part with the other.
Nevertheless, some are walking alone
and are in such isolation that they are
often less alone than the others who found
each other and are bound forever together
and who would like to feel themselves unbound
to casually walk through the city now and then,
for snowing reminds us of the rose's
shedding itself of loose stinging leaves.

HAPPY PEOPLE

There they are all rich and grand,
living on nothing but little thoughts,
the purest and best imaginable,
and they have the loveliest of gestures,
from their vest pockets they pull out
the most useful and practical ideas.
No one has ever seen them walk other
than how they would like to see them walk,
with their heads happily held high, and in
their hearts only feelings joking and smiling.
Everything there to which people aspire
was given to them by God's kindness,
and when you ask who these people are,
you will find that a child has imagined
them so. I run to this place
as fast as I can
in order to rejoice.

Women

WOMEN

There is something very attractive in women
to complain about the smallest of things,
to carry on and on about something or other,
which could just be grabbed by the collar,
what I want to say in a roundabout way is
they much enjoy hanging on to a question.
They let go of an almost deliberate
apprehension to happily devote themselves
to feelings, to sulkiness and matters of passion.
A woman's mind wavers and is soft indeed,
you can already tell by the set of their jaws
that such souls never think of daring anything,
they would rather let themselves be gnawed by pain.
A shame that I am such a connoisseur of women.

THE PORCELAIN FIGURINE

He was made of porcelain,
wore lace-trimmed shorts
and sang to her, crazed
to be by her,
the cock in her cage.
He did not fail
in his difficult, noble,
great duty to sing,
but her face remained unmoved,
as he was wearing himself out
with his singing.
While he lovingly plucked away
on his mandolin, she peeled an orange,
which she ate with obvious pleasure,
and calmly studied the performer with her beautiful eyes.
He sang until her composure
made him grow pale.
How delightful was his voice,
as I bent over the figurine,
which adorned the window of an antique shop!
I genuinely felt sorry for the boy,
whom hopelessness forced to sing.
It was as if his heart began
to throb underneath his floral vest,
like a scared fledgling in its nest.
His eyes would have teared up
had his stony spirit allowed it.
He was spared an enchanting
disenchantment. Like Heine,
as is well known,
in Paris,

who would sigh and sigh,
exhale misery, as it were,
and gently
smile on top of that.
I wrote this poem
at eight in the morning,
and I hope that you will pay it some attention.
It is not like I worked up a sweat,
I prefer not to bathe in
excessive zealousness.
What could be so important
about the sound of a porcelain guitar?
We do not care about
the suffering of days past.
After all we treat the present as gently
and thoughtfully as possible.
Love and life and songs
will always mount once more.

THE GIRL WITH THE PEARLS

I felt no sympathy for him,
allowed him to dress me with love,
I was the figure who cheered him up,
the opaque azure.
From time to time I let him laugh at me,
but only for marvellous presents in return.
He did not really know why he
adorned my slender neck with pearls.
He did not know why he adored me,
he only knew that I was his sweet light.
I did not know everything he knew,
or what it was that made him love me.
I laughed when he called me a whore,
and so captivated him even more.
'I know how happy I make you,'
I told him and used no wiles
to keep him faithful to me;
I let the unforced coincidence prevail,
which knows best how to create.
When he was angry, so I became beautiful,
and like in a föhn it glistened around me,
and I began to shine from within
when I saw him trembling, whimpering
inside, I rewarded such mockery with love.
Did he not love me even more for it?
I felt no sympathy for him, only fret
that I would no longer enjoy being
embraced by him,
then the arcs
of loneliness proudly
encircled him,
and I suddenly cared no more,
he was but a vestige of his former self to me.

LADY IN A RIDING HABIT

From her rumpled woods
she rises coolly
into a day of no demands,
rings for her servant
to bring her chocolate
and to sing to her of self-defeat
and does not hate or love herself
and then writes a letter to her
beautiful friend, the Lady of Langenthal,
a letter girdled with reflections,
brief, clever, sweet,
in which she pretends to be
at once innocent and amazingly worldly.
Finished with her correspondence,
she perfumes herself
and feels purer,
more eager, more sacrificing,
but also more loving than ever before.
'How sweet I am,' she says to herself,
perhaps with a semblance of frivolous
self-admiration, then her Robert hands
her the riding whip, and now she rides
through two-hundred-year-old avenues,
her appearance attracts attention
and offers encouragements.
Whether or not they pay attention and whether
or not they believe us depends on talent.

THE PAGE

She had already pretty much agreed to meeting him.
Then he trembled with excitement, danced, laughed.
In his imagination he sang for her a little serenade,
but a few other people were thinking about her too.
The daughter was watched over unmercifully,
during many a bright,
long silver-moonlit night, the page very gently
fans his indescribably faithful fire of servitude.

THE HAPPY GIRL

She sat there properly,
with her slender hands in her lap,
neither feeling more or less
focused on her task.
When later I saw her
talking in a kind way,
I thought: As tough as
she is on herself, she is
gentle with others,
which is why
she does not espy
whether fortune might lie ahead.
She has the silken mind
of the modest who are
happy with themselves.
Beauty has never
abandoned the humble.

YES, THAT IS HOW WE ARE

Oh, dear, young woman, so delicate,
how your slenderness dresses you.
In this loud, colourful, opulent, vast hall,
you sounded of morbid deliberations.
Your husband looked at you apprehensively.
In the grey, cold light outside,
city dwellers streamed around,
the young and the old,
and those neither young nor old.
You did not have much stride
in you as I watched.
Pale grow the pale, as it were,
before those enjoying themselves
in a life they no longer allow
themselves, who strive for nothing
but to move in a circle.
Oh, dear, young woman so delicate,
strange, we are refined and considerate and kind and good
and hard.

FANTASY OF A KISS

He loved her but never told her.
Will you believe what I am telling you:
He killed her soul with his wondrous eyes,
so that she was forced to deal with her dead
feelings, with those most highly revived,
you could say as well, and she shot him,
and bleeding, he thus retreated into his
bedroom, which lay beneath the massive
weight of a dome, and here, in the glow
of a hundred candles that were lit
by a hardworking maid, to rest,
as if on a crimson bed, on the blood
which was flowing from his wound,
and to rejoice in his suffering and to turn
his pain into pleasure and whisper to himself:
'How delighted I am with this rightly
acquired, sweet dying of mine.' She,
who gave him such a kiss with the bullet,
afterward married most commendably,
and now plays a prominent role in society.
Now she is a keeper, is she not?

THE GIRL WITH THE BEAUTIFUL EYES

The station hall is getting painted white, I am sitting,
considerably even keel with myself, crowds roiling
around me, looking at the eyes of a feminine personality,
who soon sizes me up and soon, ever so sensibly,
drops me from her view. There are wonderful absences,
presences inherent in this role she refuses to play,
but she plays it all the same, with pleasure, her soul tells her,
how much I love her two shining stars, and how much
I am drawn to her, how much I want to spend my one true life
with her, yet she also knows of my efforts to learn and create,
and so she often conceals, oh, do you see it, gentlemen,
in honour of greatness, that splendour I am unable to resist.

THE CHARMING GENTLEMAN

Little matron from the Seeland, oh, why are you making
such a worried face on my eight o'clock in the morning mandolin.
She pours coffee into her cup, while her husband
is thinking about eternity as he reads the Bible.
The married couple is a creation by Anker, our great painter.
What whimsical, riddle-posing and overly skinny figure
had captured this stock character in spite of our culture.
But perhaps there is a higher meaning in this enchantment.
A hundred times already he shook his wise head in the negative
because of the feeling that seized him, but it knocks
and pounds in his soul like hammer blows in a forge;
his hitherto prosaic existence turns into a melody.
How interesting it is when two little blue eyes
are continuously superior to the superior.

DUET

She:
Maybe, maybe— —

He:
    Why are you talking to yourself?

She:
The meadows are turning greener and yellower.
The grass, you can literally see it changing.
Sometimes I feel as if I were made of glass,
do you see it, so fine, so proud and so fragile.
Again I appear to be neither here nor there.
I am very much afraid of my mother
and I am a nothing, a speck of dust— —

He:
                Now, now.

She:
Now that I have seen you a few times—

He:
You are just so-so and la-la-la.

She:
Just let me speak, will you, you uncouth little rascal.
From the start I thought you were an angel.
And how you are now standing here so level-headed,
calm and most friendly like a Persian Shah.
At the tavern we ate salad and roasted meat.

He:
At your request I would pick up a garden spade.

She:
  Sure you would!

He:
            And why not? Do you
feel like my behaviour makes me look as if I came from
Zurich, as if I had hands only to cup my chin with,
to appear deep in thought?

She:
                    I never held
you for a blockhead. Now the trees are already
covered in green, you feel as if they are singing
to you in such a rather peculiar way.
How this lovely breeze both warms and cools me.
You are like a gentle wind as well, unknown,
like a current coming down from up above.
How the stars were flickering last night
in such a modest and awesome splendour.
The flowers and the stars and then you!
Does it not seem like you are my peace?
    (*She leans against him.*)

He:
You take possession of me very blatantly.

She:
As if this were not more than obvious here.
As if you have not been waiting for it,
for my careful and tender moving toward you.

He:
You have long been flirting with my
and your precious stones of existence.
And do not forget, according to the latest
theory, we are all but expressions of eternity.
Hence we will never be able to value each
other enough.

She:
                              Come to my room,
so that we may enjoy the glow of each
other's eyes, and where we shall prepare
ourselves for your reading of a few pages
from the Me-book you have written, in which
you describe how much you truly love me.
You will recite and I will listen; and when
I hear you speak, I will be at peace with you
and myself. Is this not the reason language
has been given to us, that the anxiousness
we are attached to allows us to trust each other
and to float freely while we seek one another.

He:
How right you are, my lovely life!

SONNET ABOUT A VENUS BY TITIAN

Her black hair looks like it is singing,
her limbs shine white with the lustre of cream,
as if the gracious body itself sensed
that it is the tender sum of sweet sounds.

She lies as if her length were pleading,
supported by some kind of ottoman,
as if she were a slender-grown flag
obligingly sagging down to the people.

A bouquet of violets smiles in her hands,
to release its fragrance for the beholder,
the maid kneels obediently before the altar.

Oh, just one more glance at her hair now,
and one more glance at the wonderful
depiction of humility in her lovely loins.

GIRLS

One of the two girls appears
to be a delicate thing like a side salad
full of fragrant and tender leaflets
and has the nicest, smallest calves
and she quietly looks out the window
into the country house of the morning.
The other girl's hair is frizzy,
like a ruffled bouquet of flowers.
The one is standing irrefutably
virginal and nonchalant
on manifestly fine-boned legs,
wearing a corselette in sunlight.
The other kisses and whispers: 'You!'
Unable to think properly any longer,
she trembles, sizzles, blazes, phews
with a passion that reaches her shoes
and a heart that races on without rest.
The first knows nothing of the pleasures
for which every girl must pay,
with every breath she resembles
a pitcher filled with ecstasy.
The second is sinfully, piously,
lecherously engulfed in flames.
Radiant with immodesty,
she was unable to escape them.
How happy and blissful is the life
that will gladly lift us from ourselves.
It is surely for this, is it not, that we are
stuck in our bodily needs instead
of floating in aspirations not torn down
like vines that put forth leaves
and pretend all is well on their poles.

THE SHY ONE

She could lose herself in him,
he had fine morals and manners,
these not merely for decoration,
they were acquired and inborn,
his from head to toe.
No one could plead like him
nor flash such spears for eyes,
daily she had to ask herself, who
was he, whether he rose
from the sea, why he was graced
with such independence and charm.
Every one of her gestures delighted him,
she was allowed to sit, allowed to walk,
so as to see herself forever adored,
to her he was this mild föhn wind,
his thirst for her made her beautiful,
she could fairly fan herself
with his love-struck smile.
Not very thoughtfully, oh, no,
he remained faithful to her,
his devotion resembled a finely polished stone,
love just simply entered and left him at will,
and he sipped her affections like wine.
She never dared ask him whether
he could seriously put up with her,
he was a good-for-nothing to her,
this emperor of her soul's light,
thus you saw her stagger, wander
off with someone else.

THE DEPARTMENT STORE SALES GIRL

Her father gave her Latin lessons,
which surely was more than unusual.
Later she got caught up in various intrigues.
Did she not wear a hat on her head,
which looked very much like a pot?
Her coat she buttoned with a single button.
She was beautiful and well-read like a dream.
With a book on the edge of her dress,
she occasionally sat beneath a tree.
Let us not waste any words on the fact
that she enjoys to take multiple walks.
A little dog followed her on all fours.
Did she not work in a department store,
with its daily coming and going?
It seems she was not very much put out
that a salesclerk might do her harm
in sanguine fantasies for her,
for her boss had warmed to her too.
'You are all on your own, so
it is with the greatest pleasure
to dote on you,' he said cunningly.
'That I am adored by an utterly worthless
wretch,' she replied, 'does not get in my way.'
A smile suddenly brightened her face.

THE SLEEPING ONE

Shall I carefully pull back the curtains
before your eyes, to lead you to something
fanciful, which the forest accommodated?
The fir trees stand with a grand allure,
slender and pale with evening like folding doors,
as if the forest were now a large hall
and dreaming of the faded echo of bird sounds.
Would it be worth it for you now
to witness
how I, without regard to their pleas,
lay the girl down on the moss?
There seems to be no path passing
through the hedge to this beautiful image,
which I was allowed
to unfurl before your eyes.
Only squirrels, rabbits, crows and deer
can be allowed to come visit her
on tiptoe.

THE MAID SPEAKS TO HER MISTRESS

How he has changed so much,
his hat now lacks its colourful ribbons,
everything happens in such a quiet way now.
But what did I want to speak to you about?
I most certainly must applaud you
for your composure, but you expect
me to complain now, well, let me
shed some light on this grim situation,
and look, she is beaming! Imagine
I had a husband who is always pleased,
who is always amused, happy,
nothing could ever bring him down,
he always knows how to help
himself by steadily facing the rising
and falling wave, on and on,
never fails to maintain his balance,
he copes with what is here and there,
without my ever extending a helping hand.
Even though it is in my nature to console,
the pain this man causes me is like an ocean,
it never grows dark around him, he does,
now and then,
consider me a light with all that I am,
but what a burden to deal with a know-it-all.

THE DANCER FULLER

I believe it is possible
that a neat little poem
wants to spring up;
she, who once delighted us
with her dance, her shimmering,
fiery folderol, now lies still;
her superb training dazzled;
yes, I will own up to it,
I saw her as well, standing
on her slender pair of legs,
whose grace she seems to have
borrowed from the deer;
flames flashed across
her face like fantasies.
Since then many a nice,
much acclaimed operetta
was staged in pretty Vienna.
Imagine her like the sun,
whose rays smiling gentlemen
and ladies came to admire,
who can no longer hear anything,
for death chose her for itself.

THE FIVE VOWELS

When I first saw the soft one,
we were close in every possible way,
to me she resembled a sky-blue A.

Then one day I came by
to an enchanting, graceful fairy,
in her I became acquainted with the E.

No way could I be untrue; no way;
I asked myself a thousand times in vain: 'Why
is that so? Does poetry not demand I?'

How I felt loveless, thoughtless
and rude, to have hurt my love so
with tender feelings as befits an O!

I said to the forsaken: 'Leave me be
with your demands, enough from you,'
and carried myself up and away like a U.

THE SOCIETY GIRL

I do believe that I am better off than her,
she who in the coy years of her youth
scarcely ever sought out a future husband,
but it is not like she was allowed anyway,
for such behaviour was not seen as proper.
In old-fashioned parlours lie fine hope chests,
pictures of men and women from times past,
with these long-lost sage faces
that no longer guide us into history,
and many amicable and cheerful ways exist,
and she is someone who knows no ways,
no goals, not even herself, and wants to be led
by the hand, and yet it happens that she thinks
on her own in all of her not-knowing-herself.
As though she were stuck in a void,
she walks by her mistress's side.
As I have met both of them before,
I politely bowed down before the old woman
and quickly walked past the young woman's
icy manners, happily rejoicing in my freedom.

MAN AND WOMAN

Yes, he was a good man,
he criticized her on principle,
it is ideal to have sound beliefs,
but not always very enjoyable.
He certainly sensed her utter
lack of character splendidly well.
She was funny, he was real.
An absolutely perfect cad,
deep down inside he hated her,
which did not work out for him.
Oh, if only he had been in love
with the capricious besom,
which is what girls are often called,
she always called him a brute.
My God she did unfortunately.
Constantly he had something
to complain about the fair lady;
to sharpen his wit on her seemed
to be his only purpose in life,
but he fought her in vain,
her hands, her lips turned
into sharp crags for him,
he apparently had no idea
that he was to fall for her.

BOOK COVER POEM

He did not allow her to go with others,
even though he hardly wanted to see her,
sometimes she choked on her own breath,
as she no longer knew what she wanted.

She just wants to experience something,
she only half lives with her husband,
of whom she tells herself with gallant
anger that he cannot possibly love her.

He treasures her only for decoration,
what does his pretty thing get?
She watches him apply himself to his work,
and no one is able to change his mind.

As she can no longer delight him,
she turns her fair back on him,
she lives, guarded by jealousy,
as if at the bottom of a gorge.

O God, so beautiful and alone,
what a humiliation this must be!
A trashy book's cover image gently
made me write this short poem here.

RENOIR

In my sphere of activity
I suddenly think of a painting;
years ago it hung in the Sezession,
it had such charming soft shades.
It was the image of a woman; from her
white dress, a broad, black ribbon, painted
unbelievably snug, fell like a feast
for the eyes to the feet of this sweetheart.
A pretty hat covered her hair,
which was of I do not know what colour.
The skirt touched the forest floor
with its hem; I had hardly started
writing poems back then;
it was spring; birds of the capital
were singing sweetly in the streets,
it sounded like sipping wine.
A decorous and somewhat demure
group of people strolled through
the exhibition hall; soon many of them
gathered before the forest, which seemed
to smile and greet them like a dream;
they whispered: 'We love it.'
The image sent forth harmonious sounds
into Sunday's delightful hustle and bustle.
If I were only able to lend
to this peacefulness the right
expression now, this calm,
from head to toe.
How nice I would feel,
and how happy I would be about it!

GENOVEVA

How come no one spoke up for her,
would not one help the woman out?
He, who was no longer at one with her,
saw his hair turn grey in short hours,
and he did not speak a word, and the others
lived to see themselves upon his silence.
With the banishment from her present setting,
the outcast was overcome by peacefulness.
Did she not have it good with her husband,
who was marked by a thousand whims?
He probably very much longs for her
just now, she thought, and with a clip
coyly put up her hair in the wilderness
and resembled her portrait in the forest.

MANON

He fell at her feet,
she whispered: 'I atone.'
The good lad that he was,
spoke: 'Rouse yourself, my sweet.'
She smiled almost majestically:
'It all had to happen this way.'
He whispered: 'You drive me crazy.'
She extended her hand for his kiss.
'I will defile you with my homage,'
he said, for it seemed
he was her faithful admirer.
Despite her humiliation, to him
she was still beautiful and young,
and he would always be compelled
to stay faithful to his precious.

THE PHONY

He was still alive somewhere,
the dog, as she called him hatefully.
He is probably still happy,
the one she destroyed, wide-eyed,
senseless, she walked the streets,
like a flower's tragic beauty.
Oh, if she had only killed him,
cried over his coffin in theatrical shock!
And her phoniness, as if she were
a poor, lost child, hurt her very much,
like something spoiled inside her.
She would have felt admired and thus flattered,
had she only found him enchantingly handsome.

SHE AND I

This girl did not think she was very smart,
she resembled a jug filled to the brim
in her self-satisfaction and self-approval.
Not in any way did she think herself wise,
she was much too timid and quiet for that.
Once in a while a tear emerged from her eyes,
and I too often see myself as not very happy.
She was too tolerant for genuine crying,
her years forbid her to be indelicate,
her little tear said: 'You shall not
think that I am not able to cry.'
I feel the same; whenever I am sad,
it just does not make much sense.
She accepted life for what it was,
I am quite familiar with this kind
of deceit as well; one day the girl,
busy with her embroidery, looked at me,
and she did so in quite a proper way.
I too look at the people in this manner,
and I find it extremely important
that nobody can blame me for much,
my life's paths will remain neat and pretty.

HOW NICE IT WAS YESTERDAY

How beautiful the children seemed to me yesterday!
As I walked up and down under the trees,
I thought about a girl with whom I
once sat with intimately by lamplight,
who had invited me to dedicate my life
to her: 'I want to be happy!' I offered her
my camaraderie patronizingly
in a somewhat tacky and fatherly way.
I avoided her, assiduously started to write poems.
It is a shame that I did not attend to her wish,
we could have been so very childishly happy.

AS IS RIGHT AND PROPER

The beautiful one basically did nothing
but smile from dawn till dusk,
let herself be fanned by her maid.
The same was very strict with herself,
she never yielded to immodesty,
she desired nothing but to serve,
having all that industry of the bees.
The graceful one did nothing
but be happy from dawn till dusk,
the servant was a soul,
as one might say, without flaw.
The other one coyly went
on walks in the sunshine.
Here and there getting blamed for something,
cleaning and nestling and bending down,
the modest one was quite delightful.
The lady did nothing but
whatever she felt like all day.
The maid did her knitting,
pleased with her work,
as if it were the proper thing to do.

THE INDULGENT

He still came to see her somewhat often,
because he relished her shyness,
but he already took long breaks,
and when he was there, he made her crazy,
but she never expressed one syllable of complaint.
What he had done for her one day,
she kept most dear to herself,
as if it continued to remain precious.
He liked taking cheap shots,
dared to joke around in her presence,
yet she still continued to find
new reasons to stay faithful to him,
and when the fun-loving husband
no longer needed her more and more,
and everything happened the way it did,
she never blamed him for any of it.
The good spirit blooms on
and on in the cheerful mind.

THE DANCER

You looked from below
at her skirt's colourful,
nerve-tingling trimmings.
What you did almost
adoringly joined, as it were,
a gesture from the streets;
the shoes and stockings she wore
corresponded with the contours
of mockery on her pretty face,
she seemed like the light
of sparkling pleasures.
Many wasted valuable time
with the endearing creature,
you loved her dress's faux buttons.
Every move she made became
such an event that you thought
she was a wonderful specimen.
Her hair was marvellous.
And you enjoyed the fact that
she came from a foreign land.
You dedicated entire days to her,
as if you were listening to a myth.
Is frivolousness really of such merit
that you so seriously care about it?

THE YOUNG BENEFACTRESS

She arrived by car and entered
the room wearing a perfumed dress,
with her benevolent hands,
to do good for the people she found
gathered there. She stood gracefully
and from her hat a ribbon fell softly,
outside the green countryside shone.
The needy who knelt before her
were much taken in gratitude.
How moving it is to present something.

SIREN

She always had a certain way of thinking
that God would quietly lead her steps.
Often she held her head up in her hands
and watched the mouldy wall
of her bedroom damp with age.
In the middle of summer she felt the cold
of winter, and in winter she felt warm.
She had a beautifully formed arm,
lovely views shone before her eyes,
lacking the attainment of any pitch,
she sang and did so with her cheeks,
which nature made so very soft,
her vulnerability alone sang on its own,
so that passers-by absorbed in her,
not being hauntingly beautiful, she never
mentioned her name, she barely knew herself.
The people told her that she was a siren
and never thought about her own yearning.

ELOPEMENT

The other day I read that a
gentleman entered a room,
where, with the knitting and sewing,
you could see this woman
in her small room's confinement
as the primness incarnate.
Yet not once in her life
did she not pay heed
to morality and prudery.
Now she smiled softly
and thus was already
someone else; with pleasure
she acquiesced to his charm.
When two come together,
they happily stroll around
until in the evening star after star
appears in the vault of heaven.
Beneath a fragrant tree
they kissed, they stood for a while,
breast to breast and cheek to cheek.
Through the provincial pettiness
of the novella they were living,
you saw them exalted, high
stepping for the train station.
She did not long to return
to the pots and pans that
imprison a woman's soul,
rather she took her chance
to run off with someone tender.

THE MAID

She served her master faithfully,
and on one beautiful Sunday morning,
she bedded down in the fragrant hay
without even the slightest of worries.

The sky above the dreaming maid
resembled a blue canopy.
A small hill far in the distance
regarded her with affection.

There was a sound very close by,
but she could not hear any of it,
and when she thought about her life,
she no more than smiled gently.

The small leaves surrounding her
in the cheerful sunshine did likewise.
The little birds and tiny gnats
can be made happy with very little.

Literature

LITERATURE

They say today literature is,
as I sometimes also tend to think,
all but a watch that ticks along
and only pretends to be on time.

There are plenty of good books,
and a growing number of oeuvres,
but sadly there is not much there
of this and of that in the throng.

'When it is something, it is nothing,
will it be worth reading any?'
they say with a worried face
for far too many editions.

As a general rule you will find,
superficially and conveniently,
that this or that book author
is nothing more than a boor.

Yes, good old literature,
nobody likes to admit it,
but no matter how far it runs,
today it basically just limps along.

POEM ABOUT PAUL VERLAINE

A small child is crying
fat, silly, stupid tears;
the sun shines.
A man thinks
he forgot something important
and is now wholly resolved
to find it; with his fancies
he could lose himself,
he goes on a quiet walk for now.
He is not alone,
but he does not know how.
Is it her, who never ceases
to manifest herself inside him?
There is a blue glow above Paris.
In his ingenious poet's room,
Paul Verlaine sits or reclines
and continues to write poems
with the scowl of an Asian cat
that goes meow for us.
Although he mends his own pants,
his works bloom like roses,
and he remains one of the most important Frenchmen.

RILKE

In a desolate castle,
where you were sort of banished,
you still undertook a few rides
on the steed known as Pegasus,
engulfed by landscape's mood,
likely contending all too seriously
with discerning youths.
Peace be yours
now, you ornament
in the great hall of poets,
shining fruit in a nice-shaped bowl.
It is nice when the job is done,
you warrior for poetry,
such undisturbed rest
freed from life's walking shoes.
At your grave
I enjoyed speaking these few words.

GEORG BRANDES

Bulletins were being passed around,
in which was printed the name of the man
who finally found his way to the great army.
The news was not delivered by a messenger,
in order for humanity's champion to be
raised up high by cherubs on a ladder.
The eternally youthful life continues.
At the biers of the famous,
busy humanity never stands still.
Imploring eyes
suck stimulation one after another.
Whoever wants to be worth one's salt
must only understand life and death,
must never strike against nature.
Even back when I was working as a young bank clerk,
all of my eager thoughts of action
sank down at the feet of women,
the sound of his deeds
reached my ears from far away.
I read poems by Richard Dehmel,
offered myself as a footstool to a beautiful woman.
On such exuberance,
     on August Bebel and Herman Bang,
     who as we all know were all
     the rage about thirty years ago,
is based my current praise,
with which I think
I must not have achieved a great feat?

KLEIST

Kleist travelled with the engraver Lohse
through Frankfurt and Basel all the way to Thun.
His mind appealed to him: 'You need to rest.'
The rose of his existence seemed torn.

To the swollen mountain stream he said: 'Roar!'
His plans for new works kept him busy now,
he rummaged in the coffers of his mind
for some unusually great subject.

Often he put his tired head in his hands
and observed the idyllic countryside,
as though utterly mad to himself.

Bemused by the dramatic clash,
a fair maiden confused him as well,
standing apprehensively beside him.

THE AFFRONTED CORRIDOR

A wide and bright corridor
conspired against me,
I cost it fame and crape,
which is why I lost its mercy.
What a great fool I was,
such that I undertook to pull
it by the ears,
now I lie here in the grave
of a corridor's disgrace,
I pinched the calf
of reputation's
person,
oh, what a shame!
It seems its
spaciousness does nothing
but accuse me far and wide,
I can barely stand
not saying anything to it.
It is silent in its import,
it wants to be relentless,
making no sound
for a hundred years,
such that I fear
its bright and wide
resolve.
How its keen insult hurts me,
I leap like a deer into the open,
fearing that I shall be devoured
by what has lost all love, joy, kindness.
The spoiled never forget!
When you look fondly upon them,

oh, that is when they truly begin
to sulk and huff and roll their eyes,
in this state, in being too full,
they no longer seek to be good.

HARDEN

Stupidities are not always stupid,
what is straight is sometimes crooked,
and in a charming cell
on Crooked Street lived a girl,
who hardly still belonged to all
that existed in humanity's hall,
and on the wide Kurfürstendamm,
standing blatantly at attention,
I greeted the man
who once redirected the 'future'
and ruled his realm with brilliant skill.
What success was granted to him
regarding the things he wrote down!
He wore only the finest
when it came to his wardrobe,
and where he has now landed,
the place we will all go to, reminded me,
as I took it to heart, of how much
I liked his face. Whether he was deep down
a romantic is a question that I
will not complete with my mouth
in today's fleeting hour.

HAUFF

A tutor to children puny and refined,
he dreamt up many well-behaved fairy tales,
of which to this day not even a single syllable
has been forgotten, no matter how short,
by the world of readers, oh, certainly not.
What he invented in the glow,
the brightness of sun and lamp, is almost
like a holy shrine of precious objects.
No matter whether it is spring, fall or snowing,
whether you buy or borrow his works,
which are most definitely intellectualistic,
as a poet he remained as pure as a jewel.

THEODOR KÖRNER

Today they laugh about him.
He quit his sparkling achievements
and dedicated himself to the common.
It would almost seem as if he had
an all too delicate discretion.
As a poet he offered a racy style,
his exertions were lauded, sung
with gushing praise by pretty lips.
Instead of nicely feasting on his
silky-smooth existence,
in a very manly fashion he preferred
to suffer in a most boyish way.
Did he not behave like a fool,
and was it really necessary? No,
another one could have been brave
in his place, but he obviously must have
felt a calling; I find him delightful
and his modest work exhilarating.
With this my humble salute,
he was unbelievably German!

TO GEORG TRAKL

In some foreign land I would
read you, or even at home,
and always your verses would be
a feast, and in a very
unambiguous sense there came into my room,
luminous with light and with the shimmer
of those wonderful words you found,
not a single sombre thought.
As though dressed in a flattering robe,
I found myself in the gorge of reading,
in the pursuit of the beauty of your being,
which is swan and boat and garden and the scent
that rises from it, you, soft, leafy,
ineffably soulful oak,
fallen boulder, the flick
of a mouse tail, a little daughter's dance,
a despairing giant, here on a Jura meadow
I dedicate, playfully, dreamlike, this
speech to your genius.
Did Hölderlin's Fates sequellent
sing to you and destine your golden madness
in your cradle and on your life's path?
When I read your poems, I feel as if
I am being born away by a magnificent chaise.

THE COMPANION

You knew exactly that it was me
and no one else you sat across from,
once, twice, several times you recognized
me and delighted in my not-knowing-you,
in the ignorance that saw you as just anyone,
someone who arrived out of the blue,
any tender fils de famille.
The coffeehouse was filled with patrons,
undisturbed, you were allowed to feast
your eyes on me, on my likely clumsy,
odd, boorish manner, for instance,
or on my undue happiness
to be alive, which can happen
when you do not expect any
contemporaries nearby perusing you.
None of us can live on air alone.
How splendid if breath could nourish us,
if success were inexhaustible.
Somehow, if you are what I am possibly
not, on meadows, paths and in houses,
beneath trees, I am your companion
inexplicable to your power of reason.

THE REVOLUTIONARY

You had many opportunities,
but the darkness inside you
led you down into the cellar.
What rare subject do I praise
here like a small singing bird.
I must take great care not to
force anybody's hate upon me.
A visor now covers your face,
and a very peculiar silence
is now part of your mouth.
Oh, why did you not ironically
pinch your comrade's calves,
rather than gain your laurels
as a man of freedom in every piece.
For many years now freedom
has been indifferent and distracted.
With the help of its beautiful eyes,
which are perfect tools to charm with,
many have already made the female
an object of scorn and derision.
You spoke words that did not please,
were not the man for difficult targets.
Brentano was contrite, and you,
because you wanted a swift victory,
are now enjoying your glory's peace.
Being in some kind of dungeon
makes us grow stronger, so to speak.

HERMANN HESSE

Prejudices, oh, good Lord,
make up our daily grind.
One day, I saw you smile,
standing at the podium,
while in the audience pretty
women fanned themselves.
You turned fifty years old!
Wandering, many a shoe
wore itself out for you.
Let me thank you today
that you did and that you do exist;
your character seems comprised
of calculation and love,
and, yes, we do wither like leaves,
wind and sea are mighty masters,
here I gladly confess to you
that I often, wearing a white collar,
as a new day began to dawn softly,
walked home from a feast of pleasure.
You once wrote an essay
about a shepherd's boy
endowed with many talents,
who honours you here; long shall
you remain fish and grape, man and snake,
and from the path of your life,
by means of some mystical channel,
break many rays of sunlight still.
Your lips are very thin.
Please do not think I laugh
at your face in vengeance,
for on the occasion of your celebration,
I hope I have given nothing but my best.

TOLSTOY

Was he both good and bad,
was he a sinner with his blood,
a great saint with his courage?
Covered nicely by a soft hat,
smart and stupid, rich and poor,
he lived on an undulating estate.
Kholstomer was the title of an
incredibly striking and finely
made little book from the long
list of volumes which his
hardworking hands created
in a spirited and lyrical way.
Did he believe he was called
by God to tell us the truth?
Did he think he could use
his thoughts to better the lives
of the perhaps all too many,
those souls he only ever
penetrated like some magic,
like some kind of magnificent string,
like a marvellously entertaining butterfly
that has been paid by the publisher
and forced the applause en masse?
Little by little he almost became
afraid of himself and his fame,
which like a magical fragrant
flower had unfolded itself.
As a man and husband he
often behaved peevishly
by the interminable ditch
with his very rare gifts
deep inside. Was he well behaved,

I ask myself as if I were asleep?
But the influential ones do most
certainly not come along with good
intentions, and all that remains
is to add one thing: he was great.

SCHILLER

In his youth, Schiller
was full of poetic virtue.
For example, there is hardly
anything I would change about
The Robbers, for their creation
is so glorious that you must laugh.
This piece has, without a doubt,
such an indescribably good tone,
much less dignified I find
the second one, because it cries,
as it were, down into itself,
instead of being neat and lively.
You can most surely establish
that here is a blow, there a kill.
Gunshots echo near Amalia,
nuts fall from the trees,
for the land's autumnally austere,
a robber's kiss tastes tough.
Poetry languishes
for the charming miller's daughter,
who only too soon will get
tired of the violent conduct.
What delight, when misery
gets killed off in number one,
which just goes on and on
in number two, as if
nothing mattered anyway.
How plays develop with
such contrasting fortunes!

HAMSUN

Back then I lived on the Zürichberg
and saw myself labouring in an office
down in the business district. Klara
was my lady's name and now and then
I wrote a poem in her scrapbook,
by the way, she once introduced me
to a female student from Denmark.
Venetian nights were staged on the lake,
pretty evenings glowed with enchantment,
the early, cheerful morning appeared
with the most delicate of nuances.
Because I was not quite sure whether
such a description of the countryside
could be considered artistic, I read
Hunger for the first time and that other,
short, exquisite, adorable novel titled *Pan*.
Almost like a legendary swan
those books swam toward me.

ADALBERT STIFTER

A wonderful silence
flows from his book.
Does it resemble a chest
filled with valuable things
doing nothing important?
Is it like a feast spread
out on a finely laid table?
Does it resemble a steppe
beaded with dew drops,
pervaded with recreativeness,
or a staircase to the sky?
Plenty of books are
accompanied by a whip,
this one, however, is as delicious
as wild oat, as juicy as a cherry.
You could compare it to the deer
when it comes to its suppleness.
As long as I have been on this
earth, I never loved a book more
than this one; it was most certainly
written by someone with inner beauty,
someone who step-by-step
increased his desire for knowledge.
This writer and wordsmith
is Adalbert Stifter, and to this day
he continues to brighten your soul!

LORD BYRON

He saw, after he had realized
that he was, as regards his behaviour,
some kind of poison for his fellow man,
many a meadow glistening with sunshine.
He could not be considered a good husband,
back then hotels still had no lifts,
he wrote his poems in a nervous script,
every six months they sent him a bill of exchange.
With the beautiful surface of Lake Geneva
he compared the foaming brooks of his life,
which made him see cities like Venice.
Restless he went from one person to the next,
he was promised fame to stand for the foreign,
and that he would take vengeance for his weakness.

GOETHE

He wrote plays during his adolescence,
in which he, unusually free and bold,
was ablaze with freedom and painted
women's portraits hauntingly beautiful.
Then he enjoyed travelling to Switzerland;
he wrote a splendid book about Italy.
In verses that were as light as butterflies,
he described his relationship
with enlightening and nurturing nature,
and his lady, whose eyes presided over him
and whose soul made him a go-getter,
a lucky man. Once he returned home,
he dedicated himself to all kinds of business.
He saw himself gently elevated
to the ruling council, and as such
had plenty to do and loved the trouble.
Still, this exertion left him leisure
to write the subtlest novel conceivable,
smelling like a flower and its serenity
but a pleasant surprise; he worked
in the sciences, the duty chained him;
and wine he could relish with gusto.
The bondage freed him from the misfortune
of others with their gifts and their talents,
who got themselves in difficult situations.
He could, with his manifold occupations,
quickly see himself of use first here and there,
and because he was involved in so much,
what was conferred and granted him sufficed.

COUPLET

I owe it to myself that I shall finally read a book by
                                    Marcel Proust;
to this day I still know nothing about this most eminent man.

In a magazine I saw a few images of the Fugger houses in
                                    Augsburg recently,
and based on those I entered Germany's blooming
                                    commercial affairs.

Sitting on the chair a young woman had risen from, I saw you,
                                    oh, friends,
shining with nothing but your cheerful tendencies to render
                                    a service.

In a church, a fine example of a female singer was singing so
                                    indescribably beautiful,
I must admit I felt not only pure as snow but also softened to
                                    the point of melting.

This morning I received a stunningly aggrieved and deeply
                                    resentful letter.
The subject matter, which should not allow me to calm down,
                                    made me go to sleep.

The conflict between the wish to live and the need to create
                                    never bothered me for long,
nature and a glass of wine in a country inn have always made
                                    me pretty determined.

Tolstoy died of annoyance, for the life he loved no longer
                                    pleased him;

a prince of poets like Shakespeare teased him with his distinct
                                      tragedy and dry humour.

Oh, how flourishingly immortal is this Heinrich Heine, yet
                                      he was so incomplete.
Miss Society accused him of being rather shady, but Lady
                              Posterity straightened things out.

THE PHILISTINE

What? Vain fellow, do you dare
mount the poet's steed?
You do know that you need
a castle before you may sing?

I would insist that you first
become a proper millionaire;
for writing poems is quite hard,
and can only be done step by step.

Why not smoke a cigar,
which will bring you some joy,
instead of going flat broke,
playing with the lyric noose.

READING MATERIAL

Perhaps you only need to look inside a book
to simply divest yourself of all impatience,
to kindly give up your actual wandering,
to quietly spend time with printed lines,
to discover new lands that are worth
exploring, here awe-inspiring figures
rise from shadowy forests, there are
towers, there are villages to greet you,
somewhere else lovely waters purl,
cities with pointed roofs grab your
attention, and from valleys you sway
on narrow and picturesque paths up
into the dizzying mountain heights,
whose views revive you, reading was often
my starting point for many a serene walk.

THE LITTLE

There was once an author
who wasted his time
writing a lot of smart words
that brought him fame and fortune.
In the confines of his neat little room,
he wrote a good many books,
yet everything I read of his
did not interest me as much
as what he wrote and rhymed
unforeseen on a single page
with a wide-open heart
and a crushed velvet tone.

THE TALENT TO ENTERTAIN

People wanted to be entertained,
they longed for sunshine,
for funny, amusing things,
but the poets were simply unable
to effortlessly conquer their hearts,
they could not make sense of it,
it was as if they had suddenly become lazy.
Apparently they enjoyed shillyshallying,
eschewing the lovely star of success,
those who the audience actually enjoyed
surely did not wrestle with great ambitions.
Who possessed the talent to entertain
demanding crowds with undemanding material?

TO A WRITER

Gladly I would like to read the book
you wrote with your most earnest soul.
My so very funny stories are beginning
to bother me quite a bit, so to speak,
because I am afraid that they have made
many a reader dreary, dull and dead.
You, for example, never laughed it up;
you have always stepped in front of your
readership with the same solemn face,
they heard you pray with a devout voice,
and you gave courage and comfort to the world.
Because I was being funny with my quill,
some kind of remorse, if you know what I mean,
weighs on me, and that is why I would like
to delve into your work's assiduousness;
I am light-heartedly writing poem after
poem, while you are serious, and that is why
you are probably the better and more dignified
man, and all of the funny things I have written
so far are making me sombre; you too are
one of those who cannot really stand me.
While reading your book, I feel like, now
that spring has returned with leaves and flowers,
comparing myself to your way of doing things.

Self-Reflection

SELF-REFLECTION

Because they did not want me to be young, I became young.
Because I should have been a sufferer, many pleasures
                                                    flattered me.
Because they tried their best to put me in a bad mood,
I sought and found ways into such moods more welcome than
                                        I could have ever wanted.
Since they impressed fear on me, courage cheered and laughed
                                                    with me.
They abandoned me, so I learned to forget myself,
which allowed me to bathe myself in blissfulness.
When I lost much, I realized that losses are winnings,
because no one can find something he did not first lose,
and to discover what is lost is worth more than any safe
                                                    possession.
Because they did not want to know me, I became self-aware,
became my own understanding and friendly doctor.
Because I found enemies in my life, I attracted friends,
and friends dropped away, but enemies too stopped being
                                                    hostile,
and the tree that bears the most beautiful fruits of luck is called
                                                    misfortune.
On life's path, we lift all the peculiarities given to us
by our birth, our family home and our schools,
and only those who could not help but strain themselves need
                                                    to be rescued.
No one who is content with himself ever needed help,
unless he happened to be in an accident and needed to be
                                        carried to the hospital.

PARENTS AND CHILDREN

The parents, whom I question here,
consisted of a good and brave father
and a dear mother who had a good soul;
they had a flock of nice children,
whose well-bred faces shone,
and the townspeople said that they were
most certainly capable of making it far in life.
Father, mother and children, however,
survived on food rather than reputation,
which is, in and of itself, well and good.
While you go to school, play exciting
games with your friends in the forest,
enjoy books and soak up knowledge,
which can be so indescribably cheerful,
your parents struggle with the harsh tones
of those appreciable demands made on them.
Because the father was unable to cope,
the mother was forced to work more
than befits a sickly and weak woman.
One after another the children grew up,
they inherited a recklessness from their father,
which was based on kindness, and they
could thank their mother for being ambitious,
which manifested itself as yearning; there will
always be someone who has to make a sacrifice.

MEMORY

The swans that swam in the pond
seemed like flames to me, I wrote
now and then in a short and dignified letter
to my Mama, who lived far away.
The trees, oh, how deeply I loved them!
I wrote verses in a tiny little room,
the days had golden eyes on which
I was allowed to freely eat my fill.
I certainly did not feel very inspired,
dreamlike I kept looking around me,
as if life resembled a great ocean.
When people came passing by me,
I thought of epic plays,
of paintings of lords and ladies
in majestic frames,
as though I did not matter much.

HOW WE GREW

Once upon a time, when we still greened
like forests and were daringly hopeless,
hope echoed around us like bells
that are incapable of falling silent.
Feeling young is a rather strange thing.
He is young who has yet to experience
the chill and swelter of life's comforts,
he who has not yet been abandoned
by every wish to suffer and feel deprived.
I happily waste my ability to be happy.

IN THE TOWN WITH ANCIENT TOWERS

With unusually beautiful and practical
castle towers from times past, the town
where I spent my little holiday layover
presented itself before my eyes.
With obvious delight I took notice
of one country seat after another;
walled gardens were telling me,
I embellish this landscape. Readily
do I believe such whispers in the trees,
feeling in my heart romantically sombre.
Here and there on the corner stood
a rural-urban valiant by chance.
Two delightful terraces granted me
a view of a completely upturned
viewpoint, which was rather charming,
because it removed me from my reality.
Undone and dreamy I went to bed,
how wide and large and neat the room was.
A few paintings adorned the walls,
I felt ever more calm in my chest.
Now people started to enter the chamber,
and in the lamplight they all bowed down
intimately before me, the one lying down,
from angelic castles I heard angels singing,
and the indescribably beautiful face of a woman,
which seemed nothing but a poem to me,
because she had such a jewel of a face,
drew closer and closer to my face with her hair.
'Mama,' I said. 'My child,' she spoke, 'I
take it that an idea for a novel has come to you.
Everyone has long been waiting for an expansive,

subdued and exceedingly tender, loftily ramified
book from you, and all you do is lie in bed
with this indomitable tranquillity,' to which
I replied: 'I will get right to it, Mother.'

THE DALLIER

There was once this poor devil
who noticed only the unseemly.
He found it appropriate to look
at women with a brazen smile.
The attraction of their knickers' lace
made him sit and dream for hours.
To study just a single hair of theirs
made him shiver uncontrollably.
He laughed at prissy girls,
for whom he did not care much.
Women were like dolls to him,
something to watch and smell.
He preferred the beautiful ones,
and with them he appeared well-mannered.
He has never cheated on any of them,
for none of them had great expectations.
He knew to play them in a like manner,
undemandingly, with his small aims.

ABOUT A BOY

This boy who came from a good home
did not lack for the force of will or talent,
sometimes he looked confused,
like someone who hears his nature talk,
such that what he heard startled him,
that he was ashamed of his sensitivity.
The branching lines of his characteristics
resembled the slender growth of lilies,
he came to a spot where the palms
called attention to themselves; the trees
in the sand had a resemblance to psalms,
he found himself in a mansion,
where he stuck to splendid manners
and trained to become a servant,
and those who saw him smoke cigarettes
thought he was pleasant and trustworthy,
in many respects he was allowed to succeed,
like the kind of people who know defeat.

THE NOVEL

For breakfast there were rolls,
with which one drank coffee;
I can still see before me
the cat and her paws.

Back then I was writing,
on a neat flowery tablecloth,
to achieve some success,
a voluminous novel.

For days, nights, weeks,
in my silent chamber,
I wrote incessantly,
how assiduous I was!

The cat's soft purring
made me write poems.
From a flurry of moods,
a new novel appeared.

THE SERVANT

He was, with this plethora of gifts,
going from one asset to another,
and always showing off new skills,
all too well. Nevertheless, he
was unable to fully appreciate
the favour that fanned him
like a fan cooling a hot face.
Sometimes, while offering his services,
and let me say this in a word,
he behaved brazenly, and in such a state,
he lost many of his innate and delightful
qualities: most of all a convincing ingenuity.
His occasional arrogance, which did not
befit his position as a servant, caused
concern and dislike rather than confidence,
when he himself even preferred his former
joyful submissiveness. He grew melancholy,
began to age, to wither, to tremble, turned
angry; the displeased who surrounded him
noticed this and now had reason enough
to do him harm. A favoured servant
should manage to stay a humble one,
but this is just too hard for him.

EQUESTRIENNE

There I found it nice, imagining to myself
that it is best to just keep one's
soul as still as a child in his cot.
I did not think about what has passed
then or what is yet to come, and,
in a clearing of a vast forest,
I lay like a boy who would have to be
greeted by a beautiful woman and, indeed,
on horseback, the equestrienne
appeared. It gave delight to my soul,
like a pond in calm and stillness,
as if there was only a pretty surface
and no depth whatsoever below the line
drawn by what is lovely and desirable,
to witness how kind she looked from
a distance, examining one lying quietly.

THE ARCHIVIST

There was once an archivist who
resolved to tell himself he was tired,
and, aware of the overwhelming fact
that he had lost his will to live,
he said to himself: 'What a wretched
boy, I am stumbling.' And that is indeed
what happened. He was struck by a dead
faint, his legs were shaking, the weight
of his body seemed unbearable. In the
forest the summer birds sang full-throated;
their jubilation rang as though red hot.
His strength seemingly gone completely,
his soul unable to offer the slightest support,
he gave an ironic smile and was dead.

GLOSS

During a gala evening a future big shot filled with munificence
                                                    said to me:
'The way I see it, without a doubt, you are predestined to
                              nothing other than a life of pleasure.'

If in the future someone wants to, even if fully justified, give me
                                                    a dressing down,
I will tell him: 'In the interest of the bond with all peoples,
                                                    please be still.'

For any graduate of a school founded by Napoleon, like myself,
the thought of being at odds with oneself would be unimaginable.

Often you can see the reflection of a noble edifice in the first,
                        the finest of inconsiderable puddles.
How I once tipped my hat in honour of one unfortunately
                                                    long since dried up.

You pay the admission fee for a poetry reading politely at
                                                    the ticket booth.
With the organ grinder I kindly drop the coin into his hat.

One evening, in a good mood, I stood in front of a shirt
                                                    ironing works,
entreating me to remember that it once was a ministry.

When you are essentially in the centre, where else can you go?
I do not miss the important thing, even when I am being a
                                                    bit trivial.

PROGRESS

Which one was it who
revealed her weaker side to me?
While she lowered her head,
I lifted mine very decorously,
such that a colleague of mine,
as if he knew about the affair,
brushed me while walking by,
and so I had to give him my foot
and call him a scoundrel!

Was it the brunette or the blonde,
who bothered me every night
with her scared soul?
I do not like girls
who begin to annoy me
with sad faces and gestures.
There is one who will not let
anyone rob her of her control.
She is the one who triumphed!

THE LYRIC POET

Because he was very sensitive,
he had cause for complaint.
He walked out on beautiful women,
and meanwhile you saw him streak
like a wandering boy through meadows
that thaw magnificently in the morning.
Evenings he played ninepins
cheerfully with the gypsies,
but he was never a boor,
for poetry gave him
grace, modesty and dignity,
a character like a fine burden,
which he dragged through the steppe,
where a young maid fleeced him.
With nimble legs of a poet,
he wandered, it appears to us,
over mountains and through forests,
heartfelt he extolled the meadows
and wrote poems in quiet
surrounded by the unruly,
who were as innocent
as the actions of a child.
Yet as a drifter, as a time-waster,
sauntering through beautiful lands,
he was guilty and started to rot
more and more and then died.
Akin to a grande dame,
his melancholic name fits.

THE WANDERER

It occurred in his wanderings
that he completely lost courage.
'Fool,' he was forced to call himself
and could have bawled like a child.
The poor devil sat at a table
and held his head in his hands.
Yet from an utterly torn faith grew
the nuts, apples, apricots and grapes
of renewed self-contentment.
Because one thing remained steadfast
as he grew pale . . .
What name could we give him,
as this irrepressible feeling for life?

I WISH I HAD

I wish I had not yet written all those things,
there being nothing more to say on my part.
I wish someone here would help me be funny,
sometimes I feel ill-humoured on this earth.
If I had only drunk coffee instead of two glasses
of beer, there could still be hope for this poem,
which is being written now and so very smoothly,
even though it is unspeakably silent around me,
I could not wish for a more undisturbed silence,
even though I perhaps could allow myself something else.
I do not know whether I should have eaten sausage today
rather than cheese and whether I can still save this little poem,
which seems broken to me. As Hermann Hesse
is known to do sometimes, I make a face like an idiot.
Admittedly, I wish I had not just said that,
it does not seem very elegant to me,
but now I will sleep long, until the next day.

HARMONY

How could it all have happened this way!
I basked in my own sunlight, as it were.
By keeping myself under control,
I attached importance to myself.
I constantly deferred to myself,
until I lost all sense of self-deference.
You cannot master yourself too much,
otherwise you will no longer get excited.
Again and again I stood in front of the mirror,
and I resembled the fragile and shining glass,
I always found some kind of fault on me,
which in the end caused me to harm myself.
I could no longer look at myself
and therefore let myself go.
The best way to listen to reason
lies in a sense of self-acceptance.

CHIVALRIC ROMANCE

A married couple stood at the jagged cliff's edge,
the knight embraced his object of disrepute.
'We will now leap from this rock wall together,
which offers us a view of the fragrant land,
down into the queer gewgaw of a deep abyss.'
She still found the courage to say, nice and witty,
'Hopefully we will land on nothing but sand soft as silk.'
Her effortless utterance called for courtliness,
placated, the knight gave his dear lady his hand.

OUT OF CONSIDERATION

If I cared only about myself,
I would already be old and tired.
Out of consideration for the world,
I held aging to be something premature.
Because I ought not to tire others,
I am full of tirelessness myself.
I acted young and remained so,
and thus I have done something
for the love of man and myself.
With lust I looked up at the goddess,
and with a deeply felt and lively pleasure,
I let her reprimand me.
He who loves is, of course, a fool,
but something will come of it.

THE POETESS

This esteemed poetess should never
have written verse: ironically, fair
youths raised their hats to her at night,
she who is much too sensitive
and loves life too brazenly. She kissed
a sailor, who was later found run
through the chest in Butcher Street,
and all other suchlike sport that time
eventually turned into legends. I
accompany the beautiful one, for she
still seemed as beautiful as a night
in which the stars shimmer like pearls
and gentle folk enthral themselves
on the stillness down a hill now,
and never, I assure you, has there emerged
significance with more eloquence.
Meanwhile, I realized that one chasm
after another appeared, and I could
swear, if you find it necessary, that I
came within a hair of smashing
myself to pieces on the sheer rock face.
O, she vanished, but she had this gift
that kept you wanting to see her again.
Happiness does not only make us happy,
nay, at times it makes us quite miserable.

THE LUCKY ONE

People have a gift for mouth and eye
and ear, and houses have doors, corridors,
windows, and in the alleys, in the halls there
was always a lucky one, who carried with him
the mistakes of others, what a burden
it must have been that pushed him down,
but he was pleased by all this pushing.
By the way, he once went to search
for something in a grand garden.
Someone had given him a difficult task
he could not possibly hope to complete.
Dignified men and women stood
on the Altan, the terrace, that is,
and inspected him, a splendid
gathering, from which, like rockets,
emerged laughter, and on this substantial day
the stupid boy that he was broke a hand-
painted cup, whereupon at once the scenery
was shifted. There was always something
important that remained strange to him,
he remained foolish, but of this something
one was perhaps rightly envious. He always
dragged the mistakes of many others
through life, and he was being pulled down
and up, he saw himself useful and useless,
lauded, blamed and in pieces and whole.

TALE

Suddenly I no longer loved her,
or I just imagined it,
or it was that I found it nice
to no longer think of her.
The girl with the pearls had
spoken to me: 'You are my husband,'
although she thought nothing of it,
and I surely did not believe her, but
I was hers; whenever I went on a walk,
I did so because I said: 'She lets me.'
When I was in her bower,
it happened only with her wish.
How did it happen, and why did she lose me
too and I entered into the loveliest contract
with the mistress of the fan, whereupon
I was allowed to shiver with fear,
to concern myself only with her?

PROBLEM

Either I would leap through every spic-and-span street as an
                                                        assistant,
a stranger to myself and others then, or the time came when
                                                    the very best
recommendations, as it were, allowed me to casually lie on
                                                sofas and read.
It is nice when the days flow over one's chest, cleanly and
                                                    dreamily.

I would recite to her pregnant passages from works by these
                                                    great minds,
she who would have picked up my weary self before their
                                            splendid garden gate.

In a certainly delightful manner
I would then tell the good-hearted one that being a problem

drove me here and there,
and how I remained a mystery to myself during all of my
                                                    wanderings.

Might I fear that she would not show empathy as she
listened to all that had happened until she made sense of it all?

MY FIFTIETH BIRTHDAY

I was born in April in a small
town with a charming ambience,
where I went to school; pastors
and schoolmasters were sometimes
pleased with me. In a few years,
I became a proper bank apprentice,
whereupon I saw cities such as Basel,
Stuttgart and Zurich. This is where
I made the acquaintance of a most kind
and dear woman, who resided now in the city,
now in the country, according to which seemed
more favourable to her, and who drew my attention
to Heinrich Heine, whose great importance
I surely did not fully grasp until much later.
Only I could divulge the woman's name,
but why should I do so when discretion
pleases me? I held a good many positions
in trading houses. Cheerfully, and out of
an impulse entirely my own, I would leave
one post simply to afford and fill another;
on the side, I wrote poems in the industrial quarter
that later appeared, perhaps too pompously,
under Bruno Cassirer's imprint.
For about seven years I then lived
in Berlin as a hardworking prose writer
and, when the publishers were no longer
willing to grant me an advance, I returned
to Switzerland, loved by so many people
for her beautiful mountains, to persist
undauntedly in my poetic efforts.
As it is I add up to a mere fifty years today,
I am told by a few little grey hairs.

THE LUDICROUS WOMAN

Even with the most unfaithful wench,
I never ever lost a glimmer of faith.
Allow me to perhaps claim as swiftly
as the wind that I was like a child
to her and like a boy and a servant.
No Viennese has ever been more clingy.
But now I come forward and say
that I rise above unfaithfulness
for her sake by never letting myself
be taunted by freaks of behaviour
in the quietude of my contentment.
Grillparzer often flew into a rage,
they knew him and put up with it.
Lovelessness and love
remained kindred desires
and like sisters ran their course.
I remained faithful to her, but she
not to me, she knew I was a rascal,
what strange verses I write
in light of this absurd woman.

THE SONNET OF THE TWIG

Oh, beautiful Earth, you beloved, let
yourself be praised by febrile, delightful
courage, by sluggish and gushing wild
blood, and you too, you slender pale one,

whom I embrace peacefully in my mind.
You thought you would become my rod.
Meanwhile a twig laughs lying on my hat
and everything that is carefree in our breed.

From high upon the cliffs, the ramparts
of castles look upon me and with artistes
singing their way into my mood,

so as to pleasantly while away the time,
to be lifted up to the heights of my true self,
unhindered by your deepest temptation.

DISDAIN IS FUN

What a pity with those airs,
in a park is all I want to be,
but I am afraid my strong
suit kept me outside the door.

What a pity about the tea room
and about its sweet cream,
which in my megalomania
dissolves into disdain and scorn.

Yet what fun it is to show disdain.
Oh, you will find it hard to believe.
To spoil your very own paradise,
it takes a rather special something.

WHAT GOT INTO ME?

Yes, it was nice to long for the goddess,
all the squares, all the streets had
an aspect of abundant liveliness to them.
I felt my soul multiply ever since I
deemed her to be marvellously exquisite,
though I told myself openly: 'She is cross-eyed.'
The absence of perfect beauty gave me reason
enough to believe that she is the most beautiful,
for she who creates is tenderness
in itself. How my heart grew cold
in time. Have I forgotten the pain, which is
actually life's sunniest side, which delighted
me like no other pleasure I have ever had?
When did the butterfly inside me lose
its fine dust? When did it start, where,
when did it begin to drain my colour,
why was I one day no longer able to die
a sweet death for her, the way lovers interpret
death as something smelling of flowers?
Everything has lost its magic for me now,
but are there not others forced to wander
lifelessly through this long life as well?
What got into my beauty-intoxicated soul?

ALONE

In the nice and agreeable outdoors,
a little girl inquired of me:
'Would you be my darling bridegroom?'
'I do not care for worries great and small,'
I replied very gently and tactfully,
'by the way, I have a heart of stone
and so must give you a quick no.'
The girl looked astonished!
Her small eyes full of sunshine,
and such nice arms and legs.
It seems we just want to be alone.

THE MORBID

When sickliness took a hold of him,
he felt revived by an amusing malaise.
Yet, as his recovery began to set in,
he no longer put his head in his hands,
so that he would feel flattered by grief
and that a sigh would escape his mouth.
As if he no longer cared much about life,
no longer felt excitement stir inside him,
he continued on his ways like a puppet.
With his moustache like a knight on stage,
to some extent he resembled an old crackpot,
and from then on he sat day after day
somewhere in a rather unromantic office.

POET

Even as a young boy he
already wrote wonderful verses,
which seemed quite profound,
because they showed patience.
In time he learned to look
into a woman's eyes with tenderness,
and with the affection he thus earned,
many a beautiful thing died inside him.
To achieve fame at an early age
can make any man lust after
all sorts of soft comforts
which clash with one's virtues.
Anxious, he would occasionally stroke
his hair and touch his cheek,
think about money and audience,
and that is how time passed.
When overcome with memories,
he struggled mightily with himself.
The future husband had always
liked his early poems very much,
he who once saw in that theme book
eventually became a grandpapa.
He devoted himself to humour,
made sure to always learn anew,
and today we linger with pleasure
over a few of his lines.

SHE WAS BORED

The streets were too familiar,
the restaurants and cinemas seemed
as though they wanted to tire her,
but she did not get tired, no, just cold,
a woman resigned, she walked beside people
and cars, there was nothing new, the world
of gentlemen, for example, seemed old,
young and happy people made faces,
behaved in a way that represented
the height of uninterestingness.
Coquetterie was no longer worth it.
'My residence is a bore in this city
once so beautiful to me,' she told herself.
Every day she thought the same thing,
she wished she were forced to travel,
yet she loved what there was to despise,
still she found much that was beautiful
in her scorn, did not stay and did not leave
and saw herself banished yet attracted
by that which seemed familiar for too long,
people looking inquiringly into her face.

THE LETTER WRITER

If, for example, one has a talent
for writing letters, each read
as if one watched a series of images,
you would presume that he would never stop.
It would cross no one's mind that one day
he could no longer find it in him and outside
to be witty and communicative.
You would be surprised when the letter poster
falls silent, does not go on like a fountain
purling, burbling and prattling away.
You would want nothing but to be served,
amused and entertained in the most dignified
and valiant way by this stalwart.
But he, who wrote those letters,
which he himself as well as others enjoyed,
perhaps suddenly discovers the need,
the pleasure of silence, and indeed
he discovers it and now remains
cheerfully silent where he used to blab,
because restraint is something new
and different for him, something that vivifies
him and offers him a welcome change.
He believes that the daily thinking
and pacing back and forth in a room
is of such an unknown and striking
pleasantness and beauty, and among
other things, he thinks back to the writing
of his first letter, and something
simple appears quite strange to him;
the start, the beginning is what interests
him, and the recipients of his letters

cannot understand this, are unable to
comprehend the strange reason why
he does not continue with his garrulousness . . .

THE RAVEN

Today I wail like an unlucky raven
at the grave of my beautiful beloved.
What a feast of life she was to me,
and now all I am left with is this lament,
which shall carry me through my sorrow?
For I am very sorry about what happened.
Luckily in this ill luck those days, yes, yes,
those days, it must be said, were the cause
for the sins I committed against my fair lady.
The guilt is certainly a rather fine one,
it needs a weak rather than hard *th*
in order to complete the perfect sound.
The guilt is not very great, I realize that,
of being unfaithful to a beautiful woman
from time to time, and then, thank God,
all those days are to blame anyway, but
in my current predicament, and add to it
my annoying toothache, a long iambic moan
helps and it does me good when compelled
to bemoan my black misfortune like a raven.
Besides, there is no question whatsoever
that a run of beautiful days, praise God,
is to blame for my unhappiness.
Let me say this as loud and clear as possible,
so everyone will perhaps begin to realize
what an utterly wayward man I truly am,
whose lament now tells him that one's liking
is all that matters at many a crossroad.

THE SMALL THINGS

I always find something
to make me part of life.
I have often asked myself
why we live from dawn to dusk?
From one day to the next
I see myself walking aimlessly,
the heart inside me is silent,
I do not care about it anymore.
Yet, there are certain mundane,
commonplace and nice things,
which is the reason why I happily
resign myself to what is necessary.
In the evening when I go to sleep,
I think of something beautiful,
cherish what is possible,
and face the question,
what will I see tomorrow?

CONTEMPLATION

Every book had already been written,
every deed had seemingly been done.
Everything his beautiful eyes saw
dated back to earlier efforts.
The houses, bridges and the railroad
had something quite remarkable about them.
He thought of the impetuous Laertes,
of Lohengrin and his gentle swan,
and everywhere great art had already
been achieved in times long past.
You saw him ride lonely across the fields.
Life lay by the riverside like a boat
no longer able to sway, to drift.

THE ADVENTUROUS MOUSE

Early on she stood out for her charm,
her face was very fine, her hair was shaggy,
one day she was caught in a house nibbling away
at something, but she did not worry much,
she resembled a mouse in many ways,
at times she lived like a pig in clover,
here she was tossed out just like that,
elsewhere she sat merrily feasting once more,
suddenly she allowed herself a long break,
as though she were a louse at rest.

IMAGINE HER

Just imagine for yourself such a lovely woman,
how she was young and good for many years,
embraced life with warmth and enthusiasm,
happily believed in everything worth believing
in, in the joyfulness of youth, in the dignity
of growing old, and now unfortunately it is
she who day after day, month after month,
year after year grows above all things
more patient with herself. She has come
to know weaknesses, afflictions, faults,
and she forgives a hundred times over
herself rather than her neighbour, and with
a sanctimonious demeanour believes
herself to be an estimable sort of ruin.
Otherwise, one gets enormously content
with all of the above over time.

THE PROVEN ONE

She appeared in luxurious velvet,
had servants and clerks and as much
grandeur as anyone could wish for.
But how she grew wise and silent now,
she who long ago could carry herself
with such high spirits on a beautiful horse.
Suddenly she found herself abandoned;
so it was only natural and obvious for her
to defer most valiantly and graciously
with everything she deemed reprehensible.
What was left in an empty nest
was to be courteous and compassionate,
to forget about what happened earlier,
to prove to herself with what remained;
and for her obedience was best.

CASTLE ABODE

He now lived in a castle,
which now and then annoyed him,
for he had no reason to complain,
to be unhappy is a talent,
escaped from his fine mouth,
and thus did he fare on his steed
through the charming countryside,
and after such rejuvenation,
he sat dreaming at home and watched
the water's wetness, and he thought
in his impressive chamber with hate
for himself and his life so far and saw
himself trembling before himself,
forever mired in his own thoughts,
thinking could not be chased away,
he was unable to say anything,
saw the peaks looming high from afar.
If only he were able to complain
about those beautiful days past!
But he experienced nothing at all
and now was already advanced in years.
The castle itself was quite wonderful,
which surely should be acknowledged.

WILLING AND ABLE

There is for me a man who wants it all,
which will simply not happen for him,
to be sorted out and coped with and cleansed.
He would offer advice on difficult things,
feels the need to be a cunning fellow,
and does not fathom that fate does not approve
of his digging for what has been buried away.
He always has mysterious treasures on his mind,
which an otherwise reasonable fool has lost,
and he, of all people, who just does not
have what it takes, should find them.
He thinks it befits him to be clever and slick,
clever as an eel and slick as a snake, as it were,
oh, when will it dawn on him, when will it cross
his mind that he ought to admire the limits
that surround his ambition, his exertions
to love what has been granted him, allotted,
when will he no longer take so many risks,
want to do what he, and let me say it,
cannot despite every creative urge.

IN THE COUNTRYSIDE

I live here in the countryside,
my fair venturous lady
with her velvet cheeks abloom
has left for a foreign land.

To atone for my trivial deficiency,
I keep toiling away like a lackey.
Surrounded now by sandy dunes,
she resists the call of homesickness.

This colourful life serves up
many queer set-pieces.
To think of her golden hair,
how fair it is in the countryside.

EASY DOES IT

If my situation were to ever change,
such would usher me among people, well,
that would really be rather sweet,
I would probably meet a few nice ladies,
but then it might happen that I
would not appreciate the platitudes
commonly used by people, I heard
them doubt what is real, wittily question
what is sacred, and then someone could
suddenly ask me how I was doing,
and like inquiries regarding myself
would, I believe, make me quite annoyed,
they might think me insensitive,
sensitive people feel much and little,
besides, I do not want to rush anything,
and also linger here for a bit longer.

LIMITS OF INTELLIGENCE

Brilliant like any other,
he was driven to see whether he could
come across purer, more direct, richer,
but, as if he did not want to indulge himself,
he behaved awkwardly during his flight
into the beautiful, lofty heights. The sounds,
the images, which he wanted to bring to life,
were not to be heard or seen. Was he rolling
downhill when he should be climbing?
Maybe! Now he is thinking of being talented,
of Shakespeare's quiet and humble Kent,
of the hard luck of pretty women, of words,
a variety of sublime but feckless words.
Many are the brilliant
who are unsuitable for lofty goals.

MY SWEET ONE

With sheer ardour my sweet one wrote:
'I still believe in your light-heartedness.'
Yet here I suddenly remember suchlike,
those who for whatever reason
imposed silence upon their mouths.
Suddenly they are far from forthcoming,
it seems they no longer want to go
where those who like to converse go.
Is it about those who have become
indecisive and now find pleasure
in it, those unable to lie on the hop
so as to entertain everyone else?
These are strange and curious things!

PROUD SILENCE

In vain she wrote letter after letter,
he was much too odd and too deep,
with no time whatsoever for chit-chat,
the kind you find among sparrows.
She wasted her time urging him to write,
to remain polite and attentive,
for a while he was unsure whether
to just tell her something whatever.
She still wanted him to be funny,
she wanted to indulge in his blithe heart,
whenever she begged him to be joyful,
he remained silent, as if he were a rock.
Surely many have in the course of time
succeeded in playing the unfeeling role.

THE NUN

The feeling of hope had passed her by;
with many regrets she let it all go,
that which apparently wanted to escape;
she gave in to something higher.

Slowly her glowing cheeks turned pale;
the years went by in melancholy.
Due to the discipline of her cloister,
her desires disappeared into the sky.

Many go through this beautiful life unloved,
you can see how they cling to their self-love;
but for those who have been rejected,

it is a given that with every breath, every step,
they love their fate and manners and ways,
regardless of whether this makes them suffer.

THE CLUB MEMBER

He is a rather extraordinary fellow,
who longs for all sorts of seclusivities,
who fancies achieving this and that,
and pretends to live in a prison cell.
In reality, however, he is very
forthcoming and well-mannered,
he is a snob stuck in a tuxedo,
rather than a prophet in a sackcloth,
he wanted to better the world,
but he just could not pull it off.
Does he not belong to those
who have misjudged their ends?
A born member of associations,
he would nevertheless like to think
that he is not just small fry in essence,
he wants to be big, but can only seem so.

THE WOMAN WITH THE FEATHERS

In the morning I write poems,
then I read amusing novels,
later I play a game of cards,
after lunch I go to the garden
or walk through a lovely grove.
I spend my time in this delusion
that I am a hardworking citizen.
I used to play with girls and boys,
in doing so I behaved rather foolishly,
I made use of my talents,
so as to feel too well on occasion.
Now I go to bed at nine,
I act dignified and proper.
Much turned out wrong, yet now and then
I see in my mind's eye my beloved's full plumage,
her sweet, beautiful, soft eyelids.

THE SINGLE WOMAN

I am useless and misunderstood,
here I behold my limitations,
what is delightful and effortless,
what flatters and captivates me.

Whatever it may be that I find
beautiful here, I cannot grasp:
exquisite scents, gentle winds,
the pleasant, soft light.

Now I feel like a nice ramble,
striding with my nimble legs,
so as to be by one
or another pretty thing.

But sooner than I thought,
my wish disappears in a flash.
I return back to myself
and feel content being me.

HE WAS NOT NICE

He is no longer allowed to wander
through the world at will as he once did,
flirt with women and give drifting characters
in the morning light his fleeting attention;
now he lives in some sort of convent.
Its mistress put him in a place
where he can only look at books,
so that he may slowly recover, for he was
rather nasty to someone he now thinks
of, incessantly so, and she is aware of it,
she grows ever more beautiful, aware that
this is simply how things are. To torture him
feels rather sweet to her.

THE SALESMAN

It is getting hard for him, of course,
to see his former wife now.
He has grown old and frail;
to kill his peace of mind,
she rose gracefully before him,
to remind him of the many things
he had accomplished in his life.
Surely unaware of consequences,
he rarely considered suffering,
because he endeavoured to go
to the top. Noble features
arrayed his face like a lie
you welcome in the mirror,
kindred and familiar.
The one he once left
now appears to him
in a vision's pale beauty.
He tries to embrace her,
yet at once she flies away,
and her smile is like disdain.
When we ripen with age,
we are shored up by memory.
Love, for which you travelled
the world, it betrayed you.

THE SOPHISTICATED ONE

In an indescribably genteel way
was he learned and sensitive.
Each of his beautiful gestures
was in the most graceful fashion.

No doubt he loved people
both in spirit and blood;
but the latter's wishes and ways
made for a confused cage.

His body towered high
above the young and old.
His tailcoat's refinements
offered no cause for quarrel.

The knowledge he could
not achieve the goal that he
set for himself was gloriously
written across his face.

Who May Say He Knows Existence!

WHO MAY SAY HE KNOWS EXISTENCE!

One ought to make an effort
to experience something.
Our fates hang
above us all.
Since we are fallible,
we may, on those days
that carry us into brightness,
happily chase,
cheerfully say yes to ourselves.
O, whenever a stranger loses joy in something,
when his life's star is stricken,
when we see him unhappy,
we feel sorry for him.
But is it not
the injuries that injure us,
the ones that invade what we know so well,
yet the soul dares to take even the difficult
as it always does, and it resists
an emotional response
and the sharpened swords
of compassion. Our pride is always
there, even when we are whittled
entirely out of wood. Thinking
about it you will at times allow
yourself, which is naturally already
part of you, how the times trickle away
and how on the outside and the inside,
the destinies of oceans and men remain
the same, how the calm, stately roar
is eternal, thus do not by getting soft
shamelessly rob your sons,

who are your conscience,
which makes for your fine balance.
In dawn's light stand the palaces, government
buildings and dwellings, where only
the best is being sought and practiced, taught
and learned. You should sort yourself out too,
become one with whatever surrounds your life.
There are manners and customs,
and we must pay tribute to education.
The church spire reaches high
into the sky. A few cracks caused
by experience won't do you any harm.
It shall be written across your face
that everything concerns you as much
as what is dearest to you.

THE BEAUTIFUL WOMAN FROM THUN

One evening a black kitten stared with glowing eyes
of stones at a cultured man of the world who wished to pet it.

In a baby carriage lay a really sweet and well-behaved
biographer slowly waking and unusually quiet.

Once while a virtuoso assembled his symphony,
he almost felt anxious because of his talents.
A head instructor watched me cramming from afar,
that is to say, writing poems, but he saw me dancing.
That bockwurst I once ate many, many years ago
sat incredibly appetizing on its white plate.

And now I come to the beautiful woman from Thun,
who already prattled charmingly with just her shoes.

WHY THIS ECHO?

I just sort of arrived from nowhere, and then suddenly
stood still because a faint sound was like my girl
in bleaker head-downcast pettiness.
This moving gesture, caused by my pity for someone
I no longer really desired, did not seem right to me.
On what tangled paths, which are, alas, so often wrong,
do we walk! 'Come, I am good to you, and a glowing faith
still bursts and wells up for you inside me,'
I said, as if I were supposed to caress the sound
that wanted to tell me of something imploring.
Life's joys, and the quiet joys of the countryside,
walked resoundingly with me to the edge of a wood.
But that is where they vanished, as they do for all of us,
and yet once more I heard songs of every kind of new robustness.
Why is it never mute and cold inside me, and why
do such clear calls echo from my life's ruined halls?

LIME BLOSSOM

Now that the cold has returned once more,
and something bronze pushes through
the sullen rows of houses and the leaves
on the trees tremble before the encircling wall,
which the frosty weather has built with no regard
for the feelings of the happy and sensitive ones,
where topcoats already embellish our shoulders
and all of our pleasures have turned pale,
I think about that spring blue and about
the fragrant lime blossom I kissed,
while your image still sweetened my every step.
Where are
you? If only I could know how to ask!
What mouth
would tell me
the place and time
where I must finally find you again?

THE SONNET OF THE CLAWS

She too sees this wet, heavy snowfall,
she, who is so kind: I have learned this
as have all who were attached to her;
do you hear the boy screaming for mercy?

They never walked as two in the evening light;
the wet multitudes sank under their weight;
they pulled him down by his golden hair;
the lay brother sang their litanies.

She, who is so kind, also watches this falling now.
What high things have not fallen since Adam's time?
Shall we not inflict pain upon ourselves as well?

Through bloodied, abandoned halls
I watch her on claws outspread,
she, who is so kind, quietly striding away.

THE GREEN LAMENTS

I neither reproached him nor stood by him,
because everyone else considered him impolite.
Was there a better, a more demure way for me
than to revive him with a few gentle words,
he who in the dark dungeon of his passion
lacked zeal and the spirited sap of courage?
Why did I not let him feel my priceless trust
in him, when I caught him looking at me,
when he had no one to bank on but himself.
To fill him with composure as he staggered
was my duty and a dear lesson for him.
Like many others, I judged him quickly,
which was neither nice nor open-hearted:
I, the sweet spring's dark-hued green, lamented,
with a lush radiance sprouting from the earth.

THE CREATURE

At night the beast rustles in the woods;
it shares our breath.
Have you felt it,
this creature with a thousand wounds,
in lonely mountain hours,
up there in that cold air,
in this nature, in this crypt?—
Do not be mad at me,
even if a hundred mouths
inside you rail against me.
I still adore you!
All people quarrel with themselves,
climb from the peaks of unhappiness
slowly down into the valley,
on footpaths as slender
as tongues, to change their attitudes,
and each one has already walked
away in spirit, back to that little bit
of happiness,
to bid farewell to those fictitious ways.
Did you see that thing with enormous eyes
standing in the woods, which unmoved
witnessed the Battle of the Huns?
Last night I was close to it.
Now I sit here.
Trains cross the lands,
ships fly on the sea.

DO YOU NOT SENSE IT?

Have it your own way,
whether you shall
still shake hands,
or on the stone benches by the soft
trout ponds shall resemble your own
beautiful gestures and beautiful
thoughts, just like it befits the sons
of those who fell in the battle,
or whether you, blind as the wind,
shall desire to drift up and down,
not asking whether any of it is done
in honour or servitude; the Bengal tiger
is watching you with glistening warrior
eyes that resemble an approaching victor.

IT'S HIM, HIM

I look out into the night
from my narrow window.
The stars stand like ghosts
in a quiet house.
What is it they want to say,
who wants to ask about it?
Do I not get up every morning,
wherever I am allowed to live,
whatever I thought about at night,
from my bed without any worries?
Is not the strongest wrestler
a mere plaything in death's fingers?
Cold-blooded he has already
carried off many a mocker.
It's him, he who lets me love the earth;
could I love anything without him,
without this feeling
that all this confusion
with a kiss
must end some day?

NUNGESSER

I dedicate here to you, proud, silly fool,
a seemingly truly marvellous sonnet.
For your daring flight in that tester bed,
all you took with was a slab of beef.

Whether Fortuna will carry you to New York
was a question you very smartly addressed
yes, and those pieces from that cutlet
pleased your body during your voyage.

Oh, but now alights from my mouth,
which bravely dared to banter thus far,
lamentations for what was missed by an hour.

But by now in the ocean's silent abyss
you feel at ease, and after my frivolous talk,
I thought it proper to mourn for you.

GAME

Without knowing how it happened,
between them separation drew near,
what divides us can barely be felt,
as if it were softly parting doors.
The two kind and young people,
suddenly drawn apart by destiny,
will perhaps with aged faces
in a beautiful room lit up
by lights kindly meet again.
People split like winds,
and like children returning home
with cheeks lacking any shame,
having wasted much time
outside playing a childish game.

ARABIA

In Arabia the man
wears a fluttering cape.
With a romantic gesture
he rides on a marvellous horse.

From the golden-glowing sand,
like a child's gewgaw,
rises the refreshing oasis
like a flower from a vase.

There you must travel for days
before you stand in the quiet
breeze of attainment's focal point
and walk through a street.

The women appear tight-lipped.
With only some vestigial figures,
unless I am being deceived,
everyone is willingly content.

STORY

It was all rather quiet in the family,
as though every member had fled
from one another. When one wore nice shoes,
one did not look into the other's eyes
with less care. Their manners seemed silken;
yet a not very genteel something accompanied
the intricacies of having to keep up appearances.
The husband frequently made his rounds in the
suburbs as a still youthful man of adventure.
He felt the need to embrace women.
Meanwhile his own wife yearned for islands
and the like. She imagined marvellous gardens
whenever she was sitting on a charmingly
concealed bench together with one or another
of her elegant lovers, with whom she spoke
as though with a rare and beautiful dog.
One of the sons entered a mansion
at a late hour, which he had bought
for a dancer's pretty piece of property.
For both the parents as well as the children,
it was mainly about perfection, I mean,
about the art of living, and they knew well
that this could not be justified in any
and all directions. Whatever the possibility,
it wished to temper itself; none ever did.
They all blamed each other in a similar
and unpleasant way, they were basically
more than happy to follow orders, but in reality
it was quite a different story. There was a scene
between mother and child. An angry tear
sadly did very little to change the situation;
because I imagine myself to be considerate,
I won't let my poem drag on any longer.

IN THE GRAVEYARD

In distant, colourful lands,
he lived amid glittering raiment,
and now he stands in the graveyard's
flowery and green elegance.
What grand stories was he told
during those years by those ladies
dressed and adorned like peacocks,
who approached him seductively?
He is dressed in a bright grey,
the graveyard is quiet, the sky blue.
Before the grave of his wife,
deeply moved he now removes his hat.
Will he again find the cockiness
to commit to life's appeal?
A little bird trills, and a small cloud
smiles down on the scattered crowd
we call humanity.
In the temple of his soul
burns a feeling of holiness.

DO YOU KNOW HER?

Have you seen the lady
with the long gloves yet?
What you began so earnestly
suddenly stood still.

The prospect that smiled
upon you slowly slipped away
with gestures of concern.
Have you ever welcomed her?

Hanging on to me
was her caprice early on.
While bright things surrounded you,
she made me depressed.

As long as there are people
who soared up high,
she, whom one does not love,
will never really leave them.

THE NEWSPAPER

Thinking of my future and getting over
my losses with cool deliberation, common sense,
I looked down from the hill on which I stood
at the smooth water of a lake,
on which swans moved like women,
as if it was a graceful celebration.
Gracefully painted boats glided back and forth,
and the mountains bathed in their own reflections,
how the excitement of a human being delights
the experience of life and how the soul
shakes in the temptation of suffering's subtleness. Later,
while the whispers of branches could be heard
in the trees, as I walked down the hill,
I opened a newspaper.

NEW PATHS

New paths
appear, when I stir,
primp and broom myself,
when I do not care for them at all,
when I settle for what the day
offers and grants me, like sunshine,
which one ought to just let be,
not seize and tie it down,
on their own.

DREAM

I walked down a narrow alley,
anxiously wrestling with my heart,
when, at a strange hour, I saw
a pack of elegant dogs;
after that I saw myself surrounded
by gentlefolk, later I got a room
with its quasi forever receiving arms,
life's path seemed rather strange
to me, I was truly and honestly
happy about the abovementioned dogs.
They approached with arresting strides,
behaved in a curiously humane way,
the office was a lovely room,
nowhere did I see a tree.
Whatever I was experiencing
seemed of an incredible delicacy,
in this dream all was confined and vast,
the heart, before which I trembled,
the magic world, through which I floated.

THE TREES (II)

At night you sometimes have terrible dreams,
but you forget them all.
During the day you pay attention to the clear
sound of birds, and then of course the trees
exist in order to revive us,
to look to them for hope.

THE CASTLE

I stand before an old castle,
in which perhaps blood was once shed,
the leaves on the trees in the park
seem to be dreaming of the event
nobody could possibly remember.
For a long time you just stand
there, as though you
were transported back in time,
saw lords and ladies gaily riding past.

I LAY IN BED

I lay in bed as an abandoned child.
Somewhere other a musician
with a zither or mandolin recital
tried to endear himself to his mistress,
who sat eating dinner in the palace.
'Oh, fair lady, be good to me!' Such were
the words he liked to sing to her. Green,
gracefully situated ravines were now
decorated with splashing and chirping
like some kind of stage scenery.
It was quiet here. It seemed as if
a few kind people were visiting me, who
looked upon me with a smile, and who asked
me how I liked my loneliness.
I said nothing. One of the lords who came
was strangely ill-humoured. Did I complain
of something? I do not know. Anyway,
figures stood around me. The room
and its diminutiveness I shall never forget.
They were all seemingly edified
by me happily, patiently prostrate,
save for one,
who could not appear pleased with me.

HE WAS FUNNY ONCE

He used to be a funny guy, who bought
clothes, lots of them and elegant, a cane
swinging in his hands as proof he is merry.
Suddenly he was poor, that is to say, ill
and lying in the room of a friend, this room
belonged to a country estate, the country estate
was actually in the nicest part of the country,
and said friend was its lord. 'Heedless fellow,
are you bidding farewell to this?' he said
with his most beautiful gesture of regret,
he searched for a bunch of flowers in the meadow,
he was happily engaged to a young, pretty
girl and he was smiling and cheerful all day
long. Gnats were dancing about and bees
were buzzing and the horses were neighing,
and the entire agricultural apparatus
was dressed up with trees, cows, chickens.
He spoke to his friend: 'I cannot offer you advice.'
The sick man then begged him for forgiveness,
he did so in an unspeakably gracious way.
Sounds, scents of country airs
pervaded the sick room.

TIME (II)

The fleeting days won't even grant
me the time for a small complaint.
As soon as you get out of bed,
the hours find cause to drag on.
How easily time passes,
as if it used to be too shy,
obliged to respectfully hesitate,
but now unfettered it dares to run away.

ONCE AND NOW

Now they stand here,
fraught with despair,
they won't risk anything,
astonishment lies close.

One puts to his lips
lines his girlfriend wrote,
others see him sipping
on what remains for him.

The twilight in the room,
the silence all around
reminds the swimmers
of past's happy ocean.

Perhaps they moved
much too cheerfully,
now they fall flat
and move like shadows.

THE LADY AT THE PIANO

In a divinely beautiful
manner I played the piano
yesterday in a dream.
Like leaves from a tree
the sounds flew,
sons of a charming passion,
around heavenly,
first light, then grave.
It is empty around me
ever since you vanished, light of my soul.
Do you not know
how much I suffer now
because of you, light of my eye,
in which I so deeply feed?
Quick, disguise
yourself and visit me, quick, quick, for I am
barely able to endure for much longer
the emptiness of the situation
in which I find myself.
You flattering banisher of my peace,
O, do not close your ears
to what my lisping lips dare
tell you here.
Why are you so quiet?
Why, why
do I arrive at such a question?

THE REVENGE SONNET

He lay in his bed unspeakably dry,
as if he were a tight-fisted drinker.
He had killed her son for her,
the thought makes me catch my breath.

He even had the nerve to wear locks
of hair. 'Here is your due then,'
escaped from her avenger's lips.
She now stood in the quietest stockings

and from somewhere you heard bells.
This sound existed only for her,
and snowflakes fell into the world.

He slept straight through, unafraid.
He felt nothing of the gruesome scorn,
when she looked like roast beef.

DELACROIX

The slim one with the flawless waistline
raised with her left hand the symbol
of her success; before her pleated
garment the canaille lay on the ground,
by which I mean a life-loving woman,
who begged for mercy, so that the stones
of the hall, where the scene took place,
cried with pity. What was the fallen
pursuing in that moment when she
found herself enmeshed in such a situation?
There seemed to be no sign of life left
in her beloved; she lay hopelessly beside
him, who no longer made a sound.
In that moment no one was laughing,
not she, who prayed with the cross held high,
not the other one, who begged for a piece
of bread, or the one on the right, who was dead.

THE UNCAPTIVATED

How it was connected,
happened so strangely.
No one knows love.
If I were lying in the brown
forest, then astonishment like a miracle
would come over me once more.
I did not abandon her,
nor did she get away,
she and I
only thought we had,
we imagined it
and grew wild,
tangled like a forest.
But there are ways
out of this enclosure;
oh, if only I were lying in the quiet forest again,
but where would she be,
what would she do,
the lonely one,
who cannot laugh,
which is why I stopped seeing her.
How we are all
in the clutches
of this helpless evil
that no one wants to rescue
from the horde of his or her sufferings.

LIFE

It is not only from time to time that one
ought to nicely and politely give up poetry;
there are so many more important things
happening. You are unable to hang on
to the tails of the dearest of people,
until finally it is even life itself,
as if a small bird flew up into the heights,
and no matter how much you struggle,
you must willingly let go.

APPENDIX

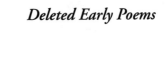

Deleted Early Poems

POEM

I run my hand
softly over my heart,
with a glowing red hand.
String music is my pain.

A lot of people are listening.
It sounds so deep, so aching.
The ringing calm tempts
them all to move closer.

And how the world
is suddenly beautiful.
How the world is suddenly
a single sound of strings.

LITTLE DREAM

I heard a soft
gentle voice speaking
so heart-rending, so lovely,
that now I am weeping.

UP AND DOWN

The earth longingly ascends.
The sky longingly descends.
I quickly walked up the mountain,
and quickly and soon I must get down.
Many paths dart up the mountain
and down on the other side.
The mountains too reach up,
but they always fall down again.
How my gaze aims upward for highness
and downward from a high vantage.
I yearn my spur upwards
and wish it back down again.
The sky moved up too high.
The earth came down too low.

WORLD (II)

A fine line of smoke rises
and it is only a line of smoke.
A small tree stands and waits
and it is only a small tree.
A little meadow bursts forth
and it is only a little meadow.
A small house sticks to it
and it is only a small house.
The clouds drift far off
but they are just clouds.
The sky is so beautiful
but it is only a sky.
The entire world is so much
but it is only so very little.
It seems small and large to me,
to me it exists without a trace.

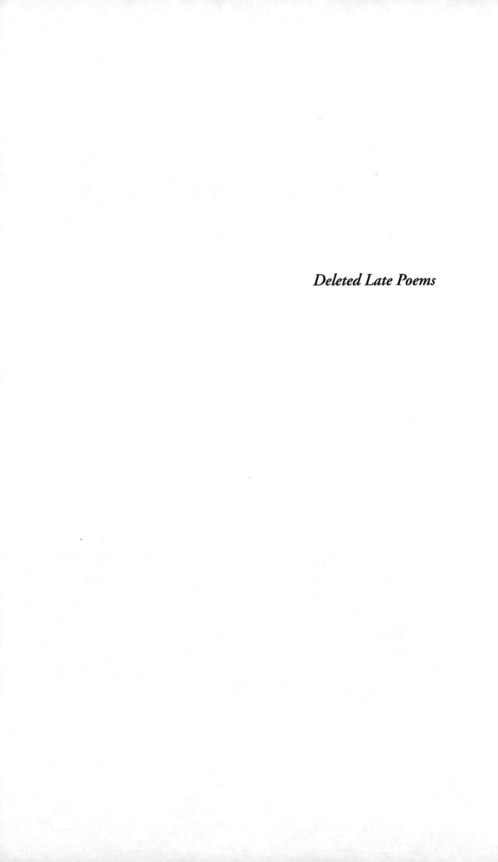

Deleted Late Poems

HIS POEMS

Now and then he thought of the 'boulevard'
he had once written about as a youth.
If I see him more or less in the right light,
he was perhaps a bit nervous as a husband,
he loved the lean more fervently than the fat,
and this is how I imagine his character.
Over time he lost much that was dear to him.
A member of intellectual societies,
circled by the sounds of civilities, fame, success,
in this magnificent story he certainly preferred
to think about this book of poems
he once wrote with a happy face.

ON A HILL

When I stand on a balmy height,
I see a lake down below,
on which beautiful swans
delight, lovely coloured boats
float along. Water's spread out silk!
What a cheerful feast for the eyes
does such a view's charm create!
But evening is already approaching,
trees begin to whisper
with their branches, descending
from the hill I might then
get the opportunity
to bow to a lady.

SO IT GOES

That is embarrassment,
they moan: the lad grows long and wide,
he no longer wants to joke around merrily,
so that they can laugh about him.

Yes, that is embarrassment,
there is a lack of entertainment,
the lad is busy with the most remote things
and sees himself as one of the serious.

He is not embarrassed
with regard to boredom,
instead of still being a funny one,
he is struggling with a heavy tear.

SPRING (III)

Now it stipples and burgeons again,
you could grow sentimental
with such lovely blooming on earth,
from little bird throats sound songs of joy,
the meadows resemble a velvet robe,
you would like to walk through the colourful,
merry countryside, which is even more beautiful,
when you are calm and satisfied.
With what shallowness
do I speak here of spring's fair spirit!

SPRING (IV)

The pretty little green grass
wants to be visible once again.
They have taken their time, the small
flowers, which you can gently grasp.
You caress them with your hand,
look happily into the blooming land.
The open air is no longer empty,
there is a singing coming from it.
Worriedly you shivered for so long,
now you can take a walk outdoors.
You say yes to everything that is
beautiful in nature and simply smile.
What else can you do but be happy
about this new growing and thriving?

SHE LOOKED PRETTY AGAIN

She had broken up with me, now she saw
me again. As if battered by her awareness
that she was the better one, the more decent,
that is how I saw her, self-conscious,
mentally gagged, knocked over by
the unsettling feeling of being better,
saddened by her sense of superiority,
which it seemed she found very difficult
to get used to. After she had spoken
to me,
she took on the same facial features she used
to have back when she still believed in me.
It is the good opinion that makes us happy,
we look pretty, when something delights us.

AFTERWORD

On 8 May 1898, *Der Bund* (the Sunday newspaper of the *Berner Tageszeitung*) published six short, unsigned poems with an introduction by the paper's literary editor, Josef Viktor Widman, who titled the selection, 'Lyric Firstlings'. Widman, at the time Switzerland's most respected literary critic, had selected the six short pieces from a notebook of forty poems. In his introduction, Widman explains that he was 'immensely attracted by [the poems'] truly new sounds', and, aside from pointing to a few minor stylistic shortcomings, declares his 'respect for a natural talent that, despite all obstacles, often safely knows how to find true and unusual words for true and unusual emotions.' That selection, as far as we know, represents the first published work of Robert Walser, then a twenty-year-old clerk working in Zurich.

In 'Das erste Gedicht' (The First Poem) and 'Die Gedichte (II)' (Poems [II]),[1] Walser writes about the origins of his early poems. 'I don't really know how I came to poetry,' he says in the latter. 'I was reading poems, and then it occurred to me that I should write some of my own. It happened like anything else. I've often asked myself how it all began. Well, it caught me by the tail and carried me away. I didn't know what I was doing. I was writing poems from a mixture of bright-golden prospects and worried hopelessness, always half in fear and half in an almost overflowing elation.' A brief profile published in the *Lesezirkel* in November

---

1 Robert Walser, *Sämtliche Werke*, 20 VOLS (Frankfurt am Main: Suhrkamp, 1986), VOL. 6, pp. 252, 4. Hereinafter cited in the main text as *SW* followed by the volume number.

1920 confirms that Walser was writing poems during his time in Zurich and that 'he didn't do so on the side but rather, in the belief that art required absolute devotion, "made himself unemployed" in order to write.' (*SW* 20: 433).

In the summer of 1898, Walser met his second supporter, the Austrian Franz Blei, who had read Walser's poems in *Der Bund*. Walser's prose piece 'Doktor Franz Blei' (*SW* 5: 212) clearly shows the influence this sophisticated critic and essayist had on the young poet. Blei found Walser's poems 'true and proper, from the inside. Nowhere does rhyme tower over meaning. Not one of the poems is modulated by a melody that overpowers the ear. Poetry is not a sacrifice to music, nor language to rhythm, or words to melos. There is nothing that could go beyond the experiences of a seventeen-year-old boy. With a certain Swiss stubbornness, this young poet, unafraid of the consequences, remains true to the localities of his life [. . .]'[2]

It is clear that Blei, who introduced Walser to Goethe, Lenz, Büchner, and Brentano, was unaware of the young poet's actual age; he even backdated the 'seventeen-year-old's' poems published in his journal *Der Lose Vogel* to 1893. (Walser would have been fifteen or sixteen at the time, living with his parents in Biel, and working as an apprentice at the local Kantonalbank.) It was, in fact, 1897 when the then nineteen-year-old Walser began writing poems. Compared to those first published in *Der Bund*, and the unpublished selection Blei read in one of Walser's notebooks, however, they seem rather unoriginal and self-sentimentally ecstatic. The young Walser certainly knew that his uncontrolled outpouring of emotions and words, the common connections between traditional forms and truisms, would not lead to an authentic voice.

---

2 Franz Blei, 'Zeitgenossen', *Der kleine Bund* (10 October 1937).

He had other things to say, and he found the means to do so by turning back to what he knew best. Perhaps, as he says in 'Das erste Gedicht', the beginning was really the wintry 'Ein Landschäftchen' (A Little Landscape), one of the 'firstlings' published in *Der Bund* in May 1898.

'Ein Landschäftchen' was one of the forty poems in the notebook Walser had originally sent to Widman. Franz Blei, whom Walser visited twice in Zurich, once in the summer of 1898 and then again in the spring of 1899, remembered another notebook with roughly twenty poems that Walser had given to him ('one more beautiful than the other', he wrote to Otto Julius Bierbaum). In 1972, a notebook with the title 'Drittes Buch. Saite und Sehnsucht' (Third Book. String and Desire) surfaced from the collected papers of Walser's youngest sister, Fanny, in which Walser had written close to fifty poems. The handwriting points to early 1899 or 1900, certainly one of Walser's most prolific and fruitful periods of literary production, though many of the texts from that period, mostly handwritten copies sent to friends and editors, have been lost or destroyed. Unfortunately, the chronologic relationship between the various notebooks, and whether or not their contents overlapped, cannot be established. We can assume, however, that most, if not all, of the early poems (published up until 1913) were first written between 1898 and 1900.

Blei eventually introduced Walser to Otto Julius Bierbaum, Alfred Walter Heymel, and Rudolf Alexander Schröder, the founding editors of the Munich-based magazine *Die Insel*. The fact that Walser published several poems and essays, as well as four dramatic pieces, in the first three volumes of this prestigious magazine would have certainly encouraged his artistic ambitions. In 1904, Heymel's Insel Verlag published Walser's first book, *Fritz Kocher's Aufsätze* (Fritz Kocher's Essays), but several years of sluggish negotiations meant that Walser's effort to publish both a collection of poems and a book of dramatic pieces were fruitless. It must be said, however, that Heymel was quite supportive of Walser's work, unlike Insel's director of publishing, Anton Kippenberger. In addition to the magazine *Die Insel*, Walser's poems appeared in Blei's *Die Opale*, the weekly journal *Der Samstag*, the Berlin-based *Schaubühne*, and Julius Zeitler's *Deutscher Almanach auf das Jahr 1907*. In 1905–06, Walser settled in Berlin and dedicated most of his time to the writing of prose. Only after the publication of two novels with Bruno Cassirer did Walser decide, again, to publish a collection of poems. It appeared in 1909, 'perhaps too pompously', as he says in 'My Fiftieth Birthday', as a limited-edition quarto (300 copies), 38 pages long, with 16 fine etchings by Walser's brother, Karl, printed on real Bütten paper. The subscription price was set at thirty marks.

Widman published a kind and respectful review of Walser's collection (he found, with only a few exceptions, the same poems he had read in the notebook in 1898) in the *Sonntagsblatt* (21 March 1909). In essence, the collection serves as a showcase of the majority of poems Walser had published over the previous ten years. Bierbaum also wrote a review, for the Vienna-based *Zeit* (11 April 1909), in which he compares Walser to Verlaine, and confirms the mixed reviews Walser's collection had received: 'When I point to Walser's poems (with only a few words, for how much can one say when one is filled with astonishment?), allow me to remind you that Walser is one of the poets whose work first appeared in *Die Insel*, one of the poets whose work contributed to the fact that many believed *Die Insel* was not worthy of serious attention. One of the poems even found its way into the national papers: as a symptom of modern idiocy [. . .] today the danger might be quite the opposite: Walser as an object of snobbish rapture.' Bierbaum praised Walser's 'uniqueness, which is completely authentic': 'We simply do not have another lyric poet like Walser (except for Dauthendey, perhaps), and one who is such a confident (somnambulistically so) artist of the word.' Aside from those two reviews, however, the late and expensive publication of Walser's collection failed to attract much attention. Walser's distinctive voice, subtle and delicate, was finally not enough to be seen as something sensationally novel.

Only two further poems appeared between 1908 and 1918, published by Max Brod in *Arkadia*—'Handharfe am Tag' (Lyre by Day) (1913) and the motto for 'Kleine Dichtungen' (Short Poems) (1914)—both in the style of Walser's early poems. During his time in Biel (1913 to 1920), much, if not all, of Walser's lyricism found a home in his predominantly nature-inspired prose.

In 1919, Bruno Cassirer published a second—and much cheaper—edition of Walser's *Poems*. In the midst of all the post-war turmoil and in the vicinity of a rather noisy neighbourhood called 'expressionism', however, Walser's collection again failed to attract much attention. In a review in the *Berner Bund* (1920), Otto von Greyerz calls the poems Widman had praised in 1909, 'lifeless' and 'decadent'. Hans Bethge, on the other hand, published an essay on the Brothers Walser in *Der Kleine Bund* (1920), in which he writes: 'We are looking at lovely, inward-looking and frequently quite ironic poems that are dreamy and spellbinding. In fact, these tender and delicate poems possess an inner form and radiance.'

The year 1919 was not only significant in terms of the publication of the second edition of *Poems* but also because Walser entered a second period of lyric production. The poems Walser wrote and published between 1919 and 1920 are considerably different compared to his earlier work: they are relatively long, they do not rhyme, and, like most of the late poems, they use a colloquial, almost chatty, language similar to—if not more pronounced than—Walser's simple and relaxed prose he wrote during his time in Biel. They lack, however, the problematic questioning and encrypted symbolism found in the poems of Walser's third period.

Walser acknowledges the discontinuity of his lyric production in 'Meine Bemühungen' (My Efforts) (*SW* 20: 427): 'When I was twenty, I wrote poems, and when I was forty-eight, I began to write new poems.' Yet Walser's statement cannot be taken literally, for it is problematic not only in regards to the small number of poems he wrote in Berlin and Biel but, more importantly, in regards to the year 1926, the beginning of Walser's late period in Berne. Walser's new work appeared in newspapers and journals in 1925, and the first drafts of 'Mikrogramme' (Microscripts), found in the *Nachlass* and edited by Bernhard Echte and Werner Morlang, point to the summer of 1924. In 1921, after almost eight years in Biel, Walser arrived in Berne, where, as a forty-two-year-old, he worked briefly as a librarian at the Berner Staatsarchiv. Walser faced extreme financial hardship in Berne, but he was saved twice by a modest inheritance, which might account for the fact that his literary production was minimal until the beginning of 1924 (though he did write a short novel, *Theodor*, in 1921). Nevertheless, 1924 marked the beginning of an extraordinary three-year period of literary production for Walser, which included the stories published in 1925 in *Die Rose* (The Rose), Walser's last published book. Walser developed his 'late style' in those stories, in which he blends, often ludically, fiction, essays and reportage, and combines the most disparate motifs, cryptograms and reflections; his texts turned into experimental language fields, where the trivial meets the original (sometimes generating rather grotesque effects).

The daily stream of prose also included new poems, some inspired perhaps by a mysterious romantic episode he writes about in his various 'Edith' texts (in *The Rose* or in *The Robber*, for example). Not much is known about this episode, yet we can sense that it had a lasting effect on Walser, and many of the poems reflect on this platonic/Petrarchan relationship. The various objects of everyday life, the experience of nature, self-reflection, as well as social, literary and historic motifs, served as further inspiration for new poems. Walser continued to write poems until June 1933, the year he entered—against his will—the sanatorium in Herisau. In fact, according to Walser, during the three-and-a-half years he spent in the Waldau asylum (Walser suffered a mental breakdown in 1929), he often wrote more poetry than prose: 'Among other things, I kept a kind of diary in the form of individual poems, separate and completely independent of each other' (from a letter to his friend Frieda Mermet, 23 December 1929). And on 10 June 1930, he told Therese Breitbach that 'in here I've written over one hundred new poems.' After decades of focusing mostly on prose, Walser the poet can certainly be seen as somewhat of a late bloomer.

The word 'lyric' often implies a sophisticated sense of language and an extraordinary state of mind. Most of Walser's late poems can therefore not be called 'lyric', and Franz Blei's comments on Walser's early poems would better fit the late work. They are often simple prose pieces, where only the surface properties are reminiscent of a poem; many do not use rhyme and employ metrical irregularities. (In an early draft for the *Microscripts*, we can see that Walser's story 'Das Bäumchen' [The Small Tree] was actually first written as a poem, which serves as further proof of Walser's arbitrary fashion of determining a text's form and genre). Walser's use of strange inversions, and the absence of vowels in certain words, for example, often feels very odd and clumsy—much like an amateur poet's work. Every so often we are reminded of the poems by Friederike Kempner or Mary Stirnemann-Zysset. But Walser knew the common standards. Considering Walser's removal of poetic tension, we can assume that Walser was very deliberately creating poems in complete diametrical opposition to the highly refined and in some cases esoteric poems written by his contemporaries, such as George, Rilke, Hofmannstahl, Schröder and Hesse. The critical and ironic interpretation of literature we encounter in Walser's poems, letters and conversations make it probable that Walser was motivated by a 'countermove' against the 'significant' and 'perfectly structured'.[3] Meanwhile, between the banal and the bizarre, we find, again and again, poetic beauty and illuminating aperçus, values not associated with true dilettantism, as well as a very original, albeit cryptic, sense of humour. We should not psychologize and dismiss Walser's work as a poet because he occasionally embarrasses us; similarly, we should not simply dismiss the sometimes provocative and strange features of Walser's late prose as pathological. It is problematic to speak of an illness or medical condition when discussing Walser's writing, for the nature, cause and circumstances of Walser's precarious state of mind that led to his institutionalization have yet to be fully clarified.

Walser knew exactly what he was doing. In a letter to Max Rychner (18 March 1926), he confirms not only the above-mentioned assumption but offers the reader a glimpse of his poetics: 'I find Kerr's question about whether a certain degree of stupidity is required in the writing of poems remarkable [. . .] There is something bright and beautiful and good in the notion of stupidity,

---

3 See Carl Seelig, *Wanderungen mit Robert Walser* [Walks with Robert Walser], (Suhrkamp: Frankfurt am Main, 1977).

something ineffably valuable and delicate, something the most intelligent have yearned for and tried to make their own [. . .] In all forms of poetry, the intellect is "only" a servant, and the poet whose servant listens properly, that is, listens in terms of the artist's needs, writes at his best, and Kerr's question concerning stupidity ought to be translated in terms of the servant's usefulness and suppleness [. . .] The poem arises from the intellectual's desire to relinquish a large portion of his intellect.' While Walser's prose pieces are already spontaneous creations, 'out of knowledge and ignorance', his poems are received fruits of an artistic self-indulgence, with rhyme and meter being external rather than internal vehicles. In one of his many conversations with Carl Seelig, Walser further discusses his idyllicized and 'simple' poems: 'If I could begin again, I would try to systematically eliminate the subjective and write for the good of the people.'[4]

Walser's financial situation during his years in Berne, however, would not have encouraged this kind of writing; Walser's living expenses increased drastically (his stay at the Waldau sanatorium being the main cause), and he often had to rely on the support of his siblings. It is due solely to the sympathy and goodwill of Otto Pick and Max Brod that Walser saw the publication of a number of new poems. Between 1925 and 1933, Pick published over eighty poems in the *Prager Presse*, and between 1925 and 1931, Brod, against the will of the newspaper's chief editor, published over thirty poems, as well as a few prose pieces, in the *Prager Tagblatt*.

A bibliographic note on three of Walser's poems published in *Saat und Ernte* (1925), an anthology edited by Albrecht Sergel, mentions a new collection of poems, *New Poems*, apparently being prepared by the Ernst Rowohlt Verlag. This would have been a

---

4 Seelig, *Wanderungen mit Robert Walser,* p. 78

surprisingly early plan for a new collection; it seems more likely that Walser was actually referring to *The Rose*. Unfortunately, Walser did not see another published collection of his poems during the last three decades of his life. In 1927, Max Brod failed to convince the editors at Paul Zsolnay Verlag in Vienna to publish a collection of Walser's new poems. In a letter to Pick (5 October 1927), however, Walser sees 'no rush'. Carl Seelig edited a collection of Walser's late poems, *Unbekannte Gedichte* (Unknown Poems), which was published by Verlag Tschudy in 1958, two years after Walser's death.

Sources

EARLY POEMS: 1897–1912

Poems
(*Gedichte,* 1909)

IN THE OFFICE (1897/98). From *Gedichte* (Poems) (1909). First published in *Die Opale* (1907).

YEARNING. From *Gedichte* (1909). First published in *Die Insel* (June 1900) and included in the manuscript *Saite und Sehnsucht* (String and Desire) as 'Die Zeit ist lang' (Time Is Long).

EVENING (I). From *Gedichte* (1909).

WINTER SUN. From *Gedichte* (1909). First published in *Die Opale* (1907). The original version is divided into two six-line stanzas and serves as the 'opening poem' for a selection Walser compiled for *Die Opale*. Walser prefaced the selection, which includes a total of eight poems, with the following 'motto': 'That's what I call a silent night, / a night that doesn't mind its stars.'

BUT WHY? From *Gedichte* (1909). First published in *Die Opale* (1907). In the original version, the last two lines read, 'something must, yes, something must / happen—then a consideration caught up with him.'

MORNING STAR. From *Gedichte* (1909).

PRAYER. From *Gedichte* (1909). First published as 'Nacht' (Night) in *Die Insel* (June 1900) and included in *Saite und Sehnsucht*.

THE TREES (I) (1899/1900). From *Gedichte* (1909).

WORLD (I). From *Gedichte* (1909). First published as 'Glück' (Happiness) in *Die Insel* (January 1900).

BRIGHTNESS. From *Gedichte* (1909). First published in *Sonntagsblatt des 'Bunds'* (May 1898).

TO ROCK. From *Gedichte* (1909). First published in *Die Insel* (October 1899).

RUSHING. From *Gedichte* (1909). First published as 'Kein Halt' (No End) in *Die Opale* (1907).

NOT? From *Gedichte* (1909).

AS ALWAYS. From *Gedichte* (1909). First published as 'Kein Ausweg' (No Escape) in *Der Bund* (8 May 1898).

DEEP WINTER. From *Gedichte* (1909).

SNOW (I). From *Gedichte* (1909). First published in *Die Insel* (June 1900) and included as 'Schneien' (Snowing) in *Saite und Sehnsucht*.

FEAR (I). From *Gedichte* (1909).

SHEPHERD'S TRYST. From *Gedichte* (1909). First published in *Die Opale* (1907). The original version is divided into five four-line stanzas.

RETURNING HOME (I). From *Gedichte* (1909).

SILENCE. From *Gedichte* (1909). First published in *Die Insel* (June 1900) and included in *Saite und Sehnsucht* as 'Die Stille' (The Silence).

ONWARDS (1899/1900). From *Gedichte* (1909). Included in *Saite und Sehnsucht* (1979) as 'Immer weiter' (Always Onwards).

SIN (1899/1900). From *Gedichte* (1909).

IN THE MOONLIGHT. From *Gedichte* (1909). First published in *Die Opale* (1907).

A LITTLE LANDSCAPE. From *Gedichte* (1909). First published in *Der Bund* (May 1898).

WITH A WEEPING HEART (1897/98). From *Gedichte* (1909). First published in *Der lose Vogel* (1913, Issue 7) as 'Jesus und die Armen' (Jesus and the Poor) and dated 1895 (the date was probably added by the editor Franz Blei and might not be accurate).

AT THE WINDOW (I). From *Gedichte* (1909). First published in *Der Bund* (8 May 1898) as 'Immer am Fenster' (Always at the Window).

PUT ASIDE. From *Gedichte* (1909). First published in the *Wiener Rundschau* (1 August 1899) as 'Spruch' (Saying).

BEFORE GOING TO SLEEP. From *Gedichte* (1909). First published in *Der Bund* (May 1898).

TOO PHILOSOPHICAL. From *Gedichte* (1909). First published in the *Wiener Rundschau* (August 1899).

BOY'S LOVE (1899/1900). From *Gedichte* (1909). Included in *Saite und Sehnsucht* as 'Bubenliebe' (Lad's Love) and with the final lines 'Wer ist der junge Mensch, der sang? / Ich kenne ihn, er ist ein Schelm. / Er trägt gern kleine Lieder vor / und kniet vor kleinen Mädchen gern.' (I know him, he is a prankster. / He likes to recite short songs / and likes to kneel before young girls.).

DISAPPOINTMENT. From *Gedichte* (1909).

OPPRESSIVE LIGHT. From *Gedichte* (1909). First published in *Freistatt* (17 December 1904) as 'Gedicht' (Poem).

EASIER SAID. From *Gedichte* (1909). First published in *Wiener Rundschau* (August 1899).

AFRAID. From *Gedichte* (1909). First published in *Wiener Rundschau* (August 1899) and reprinted in *Die Opale* (1907) and Julius Zeitler's *Deutscher Almanach auf das Jahr 1907* (1907).

DO YOU SEE? From *Gedichte* (1909).

AND LEFT. From *Gedichte* (1909). First published in *Wiener Rundschau* (August 1899).

HOUR. From *Gedichte* (1909). First published in *Die Insel* (June 1900).

WEARINESS. From *Gedichte* (1909). First published in *Wiener Rundschau* (August 1899).

ILLUSION. From *Gedichte* (1909). First published in *Wiener Rundschau* (August 1899).

SERENITY. From *Gedichte* (1909). First published in *Die Insel* (October 1899) and included in *Saite und Sehnsucht* (without stanza breaks) as 'Beruhigung' (Calm).

String and Desire
(Saite und Sehnsucht)

WINTER NIGHT. From *Saite und Sehnsucht*. Unpublished.

IT IS NIGHT. From *Saite und Sehnsucht*. Unpublished.

ROMANCE. From *Saite und Sehnsucht*. Unpublished.

TIME. From *Saite und Sehnsucht*. Unpublished.

MEADOW GREEN. From *Saite und Sehnsucht*. Unpublished.

EVENING (II). From *Saite und Sehnsucht*. Unpublished.

AT THE WINDOW (II). From *Saite und Sehnsucht*. Unpublished.

EVERYTHING GREEN. From *Saite und Sehnsucht*. Unpublished.

THE BELOVED. From *Saite und Sehnsucht*. Unpublished.

SNOW (II): From *Saite und Sehnsucht*. Unpublished.

THUS IT FALLS THROUGH THE TREES. From *Saite und Sehnsucht*. Unpublished.

FLOWERS. From *Saite und Sehnsucht*. Unpublished.

WINTER RAIN. From *Saite und Sehnsucht*. Unpublished.

ALL IS NIGHT. From *Saite und Sehnsucht*. Unpublished.

FEAR (II). From *Saite und Sehnsucht*. Unpublished.

VOICES. From *Saite und Sehnsucht*. Unpublished.

DIFFICULT MORNING. From *Saite und Sehnsucht*. Unpublished.

FEVER. From *Saite und Sehnsucht*. Unpublished.

HOPE. From *Saite und Sehnsucht*. Unpublished.

UNDER A GREY SKY. From *Saite und Sehnsucht*. Unpublished.

ALL THIS. From *Saite und Sehnsucht*, where it was included as two separate and untitled two-liners facing the next poem, 'Abendlied' (Evening Song). As such, it is unclear whether this is a separate poem or simply additional lines of 'Abendlied'. Unpublished.

EVENING SONG. From *Saite und Sehnsucht*. Unpublished.

PEACE?. From *Saite und Sehnsucht*. Unpublished.

THE FOREST (I). From *Saite und Sehnsucht*. Unpublished.

BEER SCENE. From *Saite und Sehnsucht*. Unpublished.

WHITE LAUNDRY. From *Saite und Sehnsucht*. Unpublished.

ON MY MIND. From *Saite und Sehnsucht*, where it was included as two separate and untitled stanzas on a verso page of the manuscript. It is unclear whether this is a separate poem or a fragment. Unpublished.

ABOUT THE FOREST. From *Saite und Sehnsucht*. Unpublished.

FORGOTTEN. From *Saite und Sehnsucht*. Unpublished.

LOVE. From *Saite und Sehnsucht*. Unpublished.

FOG. From *Saite und Sehnsucht*. Unpublished.

Further Selections

THE FUTURE! (1897). This is Walser's earliest known poem. On 10 June 1897, he sent it to Robert Seidel, a socialist politician, pedagogue and writer, who at the time was the editor of the *Arbeiterstimme*. Unpublished.

FOR MY DARLING FANNY! (1897). Walser's sister Fanny was fourteen at the time. Walser signed the poem with 'From your faithful brother Robert'. Unpublished.

GLOOMY NEIGHBOUR. From *Saite und Sehnsucht* (1897). First published in *Der Bund* (May 1898).

DREAMS. First published in *Der Bund* (May 1898). Included in *Saite und Sehnsucht* (without stanza breaks).

CLOSING TIME (1898). From a letter written by Franz Blei to Otto Julius Bierbaum (dated 6 August 1898): 'From a few W. brought me, I'll copy this one for you.' First published by Erich Unglaub in *Recherches Germaniques* (Volume 10, 1980).

LAUGHING AND SMILING. First published in *Die Insel* (October 1899). Included in *Saite und Sehnsucht* (without a title). Also included in *Essays* (1913).

FOR FANNY (1901). Unpublished poem dedicated to Walser's sister Fanny.

FAINT-HEARTED. First published in Julius Zeitler's *Deutscher Almanach auf das Jahr 1907* (1907).

TRAGEDY. First published in *Die Schaubühne* (April 1907).

THE CONCERTINA PLAYER. First published in *Arkadia* (1913) as 'Handharfe am Tag' (Concertina at Daytime). Reprinted in *Prager Tagblatt* (20 November 1927). In Bernese German, a 'Handharfe' is a concertina or accordion.

I WANDERED (before 1905). Included in *Kleine Dichtungen* (Short Poems) (1914).

POEMS WRITTEN IN BIEL: 1919–1920

SPRING (I). First published in *Pro Helvetia* (May 1919).

SULKING. First published in *Neue Zürcher Zeitung* (July 1919).

LITTLE MOUSE. First published in *Vossische Zeitung* (August 1919).

RETURNING HOME (II). First published in *Pro Helvetia* (August 1919). The poem is titled 'Traum' (Dream) in the original manuscript.

DOLL. First published in *Die Rheinlande* (September/October 1919).

THE KIND. First published in *Pro Helvetia* (June 1920).

CHOPIN. First published in *Die Weltbühne* (September 1920).

SUNDAY. Unpublished.

OCTOBER. First published in *Schweizerisches Familienwochenblatt* (October 1920).

AFTER DRAWINGS BY DAUMIER. First published in *Kunst und Künstler* (November 1920). Only the drawings described in the last two stanzas have been identified. The 'man in the pleasure boat' is based on Number 16, 'Une recontre désagréable', in the series of lithographed drawings titled 'Les canotiers Parisiens', first published in *Charivari* on 6 July 1843 (no. 1038 in Loys Delteil's catalogue *Honoré Daumier*, Paris, 1925/26). The gentleman in the barbershop is based on Number 22 in the series titled 'Mœurs conjugales', first published in *Charivari* on 5 April 1840 (no. 645 in Delteil), with the following note: 'C'est ma femme!! oh! scélérate, pendant qu'on me fait la barbe, elle me fait la queue!' The first stanza is probably based on the woodcut 'Le Poète de salon', pg. 85, *Physiologie du poète*, Sylvius, Paris, 1841 (no. 306 in Arthur Rümann's catalogue *Honoré Daumier / Sein Holzschnittwerk*, Munich, 1914).

APOLLO AND DIANA BY LUCAS CRANACH. First published in *Kunst und Künstler* (November 1920).

THE CHRISTMAS TREE. First published in *Der Bund* (December 1920).

POEMS WRITTEN IN BERNE: 1924–1933

Can It Wish Me Anything Other than Happiness

CAN IT WISH ME ANYTHING OTHER THAN HAPPINESS. First published in *Wissen und Leben* (June 1925) and then reprinted in Albert's Sergel's anthology *Saat und Ernte* (1925).

HOW THE SMALL HILLS SMILED. First published in *Wissen und Leben* (June 1925) and then reprinted in Albert Segel's anthology *Saat und Ernte* (1925).

THE ALLEY (1925). First published in *Prager Presse* (May 1931).

SUNDAY MORNING FLAGS (1925). First published in *Prager Presse* (June 1928).

SUN (1925). First published in *Prager Presse* (August 1933).

THE PLEASURE CASTLE. First published in *Prager Presse* (September 1925).

THE LONGED-FOR ISLAND. First published in *Prager Tagblatt* (October 1925).

WINTER (I) (1925/26). Johanna Siebel (1873–1939), teacher and writer from Zurich, who wrote several volumes of poetry. Unpublished.

SPRING (II) (1925/26). Walser completed his basic military training in the summer of 1903. Adolf Deucher (1831–1912) was a former Swiss federal councillor. The Kornhauskeller is a restaurant near the Kornhausplatz in Berne. Unpublished.

THE LAD IN THE CARPATHIANS. First published in *Prager Pesse* (December 1926).

CHRISTMAS TREE. First published in *Prager Presse* (December 1926).

SENSATION (1926/27). First published in *Prager Tagblatt* (October 1927).

THE SEASONS (1927). First published in *Prager Tagblatt* (November 1927).

THE FOREST (II) (1927). First published in *Prager Presse* (July 1928).

SPRING FLOWERS (1927). First published in *Prager Presse* (September 1928).

HOW I SAW A LEAF FALLING. First published in *Prager Tagblatt* (October 1927).

PARADE (1927). First published in *Prager Presse* (August 1933). From a letter to Otto Pick, 17 September 1927: 'Here's "Parade", a poem I wrote to celebrate the occasion of the Bernese costume festival two weeks ago, trying to give it a sense of general importance.'

CHRISTMAS (1927). First published in *Prager Presse* (December 1927).

THE CARROUSEL (1927/28). Unpublished.

SUNDAY WALK (1928/29). Unpublished.

IN THE HOSPITAL. First published in *Prager Tagblatt* (June 1928).

AUTUMN (I) (1928). First published in *Prager Presse* (October 1928).

SNOW (III). First published in *Prager Presse* (January 1929).

A SHORT LETTER. First published in *Prager Tagblatt*. Date of publication unknown.

LONGING. First published in *Prager Tagblatt* (June 1928).

SPRING (1928/29). First published in *Prager Presse* (April 1929).

WINTER (II) (1928/29). Unpublished.

CHRISTMAS BELLS (1928). Unpublished.

SNOW (IV). First published in *Prager Tagblatt* (February 1930).

IN THE FOREST (1930). Unpublished.

THE JOYS OF BATHING (1930). Unpublished.

TRAVELLING (1930). First published in *Prager Presse* (April 1931).

EVENING (III) (1930). Unpublished.

CIRCE (1930). Unpublished.

THE ISLAND (1930). Unpublished.

SWITZERLAND (1930). Unpublished.

A GLASS OF BEER (1930). Unpublished.

THE TINY VILLAGE (1930). Unpublished.

AUTUMN (II). First published in *Prager Tagblatt* (October 1930).

THE LITTLE TOWN (1930). First published in *Prager Presse* (October 1931).

VACATION (1930). First published in *Prager Presse* (June 1931).

EVENING (IV) (1930). Unpublished.

THE READER (1930). Unpublished.

THE CHURCH (1930). Unpublished.

THE LITTLE ONES. First published in *Prager Tagblatt* (December 1930).

JOY OF LIFE (1930). Unpublished.

INVITATION (1930). Unpublished.

APRIL (1930/31). Joachim Ringelnatz (Hans Böttiger, 1883–1934), humoristic poet and cabaret artist. Unpublished.

SUMMER (1931). First published in *Prager Presse* (September 1931).

BOAT RIDE (1931/32). Unpublished.

IN THE WOODS (1931/32). Unpublished.

WINTER (III). First published in *Prager Tagblatt* (January 1931).

THE TRAVELLING JOURNEYMAN (1932/33). Unpublished.

SLEEP WELL (1930). Unpublished.

The Child Ponders

THE CHILD PONDERS (1925). First published in *Prager Presse* (March 1931).

DAILY ROUTINES. First published in *Prager Tagblatt* (February 1929).

THE FURNISHED ROOM (1928/29). First published in *Prager Presse* (June 1932).

THE COMFORT OF COMPLAINING (1930). Walser originally titled this poem 'The Comfort of Forgetting'. Unpublished.

NO ONE IS FLAWED (1930). Unpublished.

THE BENEFITS OF TALKING (1930). Unpublished.

SLEEP (1930). Unpublished.

WHY NOT BE STILL? (1930). Unpublished.

FAMILY LIFE (1930). First published in *Prager Presse* (July 1931).

THE BEAUTY (1930). Unpublished.

HIGH ART (1930). First published in *Prager Presse* (March 1931). The first performance of *Falstaff*, Verdi's last opera, took place on 9 February 1893 at La Scala in Milan.

THE BROOK (1930). Unpublished.

DANIEL IN THE LION'S DEN (1925). First published in *Prager Presse* (October 1927).

YOUNG JOHN. First published in *Prager Tagblatt* (May 1925).

THE CHRIST CHILD (1928/29). Unpublished.

MARY IN THE TENT. First published in *Prager Presse* (April 1926).

JESUS, THE INSCRUTABLE ONE. First published in *Prager Tagblatt* (May 1925).

THE PERFECT ONE (1928/29). First published in *Prager Presse* (July 1933).

THE SUFFERING FACE. First published in *Prager Tagblatt* (December 1926).

THE CRUCIFIED ONE (1926). First published in *Prager Tagblatt* (December 1926).

WE SEE HIM SMILE. First published in *Prager Presse* (May 1926).

THE LOST SON. First published in *Prager Presse* (April 1928).

DON JUAN. First published in *Prager Presse* (February 1931).

THE PETIT BOURGEOIS (1925/26). First published in *Prager Presse* (September 1926).

RIZZIO THE SINGER (1930). David Rizzio (circa 1540–1566), singer, courtier and private secretary of Mary, Queen of Scots. He was killed by Lord Darnley, Mary's husband. Unpublished.

PASCIN. First published in *Prager Presse* (July 1930). Jules Pascin (1885–1930), Bulgarian painter and artist.

VAN GOGH. First published in *Prager Presse* (May 1933). Vincent Van Gogh (1853–1890), Dutch painter.

THE BERNESE PAINTER ALBERT ANKER. First published in *Prager Presse* (May 1933). Albert Anker (1831–1910), Swiss painter and illustrator.

LINDBERGH (1927). Charles Lindbergh (1902–1974), American aviator, military officer, author, inventor and environmental activist. Unpublished.

THE JAILHOUSE SONNET. First published in *Prager Presse* (May 1927).

RIDDLES (1926/27). First published in *Neue Schweizer Rundschau* (September 1927).

SNOW. Unpublished.

CITY IN THE SNOW. First published in *Prager Tagblatt* (February 1930).

HAPPY PEOPLE. First published in *Prager Tagblatt* (April 1931).

Women

WOMEN. First published in *Prager Tagblatt* (March 1927).

THE PORCELAIN FIGURINE. First published in *Wissen und Leben* (June 1925).

THE GIRL WITH THE PEARLS (1926/27). Unpublished.

LADY IN A RIDING HABIT. First published in *Simplicissimus* (June 1925). Langenthal is an industrial town in the canton of Berne. The 'Lady of Langenthal', however, seems to be a fictitious figure.

THE PAGE. First published in *Prager Presse* (September 1925).

THE HAPPY GIRL. First published in *Prager Tagblatt* (September 1925).

YES, THAT IS HOW WE ARE (1925). First published in *Prager Presse* (November 1933).

FANTASY OF A KISS (1925). First published in *Prager Presse* (August 1928).

THE GIRL WITH THE BEAUTIFUL EYES. First published in *Prager Presse* (February 1926).

THE CHARMING GENTLEMAN. First published in *Prager Presse* (February 1926).

DUET. First published in *Prager Presse* (December 1926).

SONNET ABOUT A VENUS BY TITIAN. First published in *Prager Presse* (January 1927).

GIRLS. First published in *Prager Tagblatt* (March 1927).

THE SHY ONE. First published in *Prager Tagblatt* (March 1927).

THE DEPARTMENT STORE SALES GIRL. First published in *Prager Tagblatt* (October 1927).

THE SLEEPING ONE. First published in *Prager Tagblatt* (October 1927).

THE MAID SPEAKS TO HER MISTRESS (1927). First published in *Prager Presse* (September 1933).

THE DANCER FULLER (1928). First published in *Prager Presse* (January 1928). Loïe Fuller (1862–1928), American dancer and actress.

THE FIVE VOWELS (1927/28). First published in *Prager Tagblatt* (December 1928).

THE SOCIETY GIRL. First published in *Prager Tagblatt* (December 1928).

MAN AND WOMAN (1928/29). First published in *Prager Presse* (December 1932).

BOOK COVER POEM. Unpublished.

RENOIR. First published in *Prager Presse*. Date of publication unknown. Auguste Renoir (1841–1919), French painter.

GENOVEVA (1930). Genoveva of Brabant (around 700) was one of the most famous figures of popular German literature. A daughter of the Duke of Brabant, she was married to the Count Palatine Siegfried. Falsely accused of adultery, she spent six years as a hermit with her infant son in a forest cave, until her husband, by then convinced of her innocence, found her while hunting and reinstated her. Unpublished.

MANON (1930). Heroine of *Histoire de Chevalier des Grieux et de Manon Lescaut*, a novel by Abbé Antoine François Prévost d'Exiles (1697–1763). Unpublished.

THE PHONY (1930). Unpublished.

SHE AND I (1930). Unpublished.

HOW NICE IT WAS YESTERDAY (1930). Unpublished.

AS IS RIGHT AND PROPER (1930). Unpublished.

THE INDULGENT (1930). Unpublished.

THE DANCER (1930). Unpublished.

THE YOUNG BENEFACTRESS (1930). Unpublished.

SIREN (1930). Unpublished.

ELOPEMENT (1930/31). Unpublished.

THE MAID (1931/32). Unpublished.

Literature

LITERTURE. First published in *Die literarische Welt* (November 1928).

POEM ABOUT PAUL VERLAINE. First published in *Die literarische Welt* (May 1926). Paul Verlaine (1844–1896), French poet.

RILKE. First published in *Prager Presse* (January 1927). Rainer Maria Rilke (1875–1926) died on 29 December 1926, so it is clear that Walser must have written this poem immediately upon hearing of the poet's death.

GEORG BRANDES (1927). First published in *Prager Presse* (February 1927). Georg Morris Cohen Brandes (1842–1927), influential Danish critic and scholar.

KLEIST (1926/27). First published in *Prager Presse* (June 1927).

THE AFFRONTED CORRIDOR. First published in *Prager Presse* (August 1927). Walser is most likely referring to Eduard Korrodi (1885–1955), who was feuilleton editor at the *Neue Zürcher Zeitung*.

HARDEN (1927). First published in *Prager Presse* (November 1927). Maximilian Harder (1861–1927), influential German journalist, critic and editor.

HAUFF. First published in *Prager Presse* (November 1927). Wilhelm Hauff (1802–1827), German poet and novelist.

THEODOR KÖRNER. Carl Theodor Körner (1791–1813), German poet and soldier. Unpublished.

TO GEORG TRAKL. First published in *Prager Presse* (February 1928). Georg Trakl (1887–1914), Austrian poet.

THE COMPANION (1927/28). First published in *Prager Presse* (April 1928). From a letter to Otto Pick (which included two poems—'The Companion' and 'The Revolutionary'): ' . . . Mister Werfel served as the model for my companion . . . ' This is the only known record of a meeting between Walser and Franz Werfel.

THE REVOLUTIONARY (1928). First published in *Prager Presse* (July 1928). Walser is referring to Baron Ludwig Hatvany (1880–1961), Hungarian writer and landowner.

HERMANN HESSE. First published in *Prager Presse* (August 1928). Hermann Hesse (1877–1962), German/Swiss poet, novelist and painter.

TOLSTOY. First published in *Prager Presse* (September 1928). Leo. Tolstoy (1828–1910), Russian writer.

SCHILLER. First published in *Die literarische Welt* (November 1928). Johann Friedrich von Schiller (1759–1805), German poet, philosopher, physician, historian and playwright.

HAMSUN. First published in *Prager Presse* (August 1929). Knut Hamsun (1859–1952), Norwegian writer, winner of the 1920 Nobel Prize in Literature.

ADALBERT STIFTER. First published in *Prager Presse* (October 1929). Adalbert Stifter (1805–1868), Austrian writer, poet, painter and teacher.

LORD BYRON. First published in *Die literarische Welt* (July 1930). Lord Byron (1788–1824), English poet and politician.

GOETHE. First published in *Prager Presse* (May 1932). Johann Wolfgang von Goethe (1749–1832), German poet, novelist, play-wright, philosopher, diplomat and civil servant.

COUPLET. First published in *Neue Schweizer Rundschau* (June 1927).

THE PHILISTINE (1927). First published in *Prager Presse* (January 1928).

READING MATERIAL (1930). Unpublished.

THE LITTLE. First published in *Prager Tagblatt* (November 1930).

THE TALENT TO ENTERTAIN (1930). First published in *Prager Tagblatt* (April 1931).

TO A WRITER. First published in *Prager Presse* (October 1933).

Self-Reflection

SELF-REFLECTION (1925). First published in *Prager Presse* (February 1933).

PARENTS AND CHILDREN (1930). Unpublished.

MEMORY (1930): Unpublished.

HOW WE GREW (1930). Unpublished.

IN THE TOWN WITH ANCIENT TOWERS. First published in *Prager Presse* (August 1927). Walser is referring to the Swiss town of Nidau near Biel, where Walser's father lived from 1902 until 1904.

THE DALLIER. Unpublished.

ABOUT A BOY (1930). Unpublished.

THE NOVEL. First published in *Die literarische Welt* (August 1930). Walser is referring to his novel *Geschwister Tanner* (The Tanners), which he wrote in Berlin.

THE SERVANT (1930). Unpublished.

EQUESTRIENNE (1930). Unpublished.

THE ARCHIVIST (1930). In 1921, Walser was an assistant archivist at the Public Record Office of the Canton of Berne. Unpublished.

GLOSS. First published in *Neue Schweizer Rundschau* (July 1927). From 1888 until 1892, Walser attended the Progymnasium der Stadt Biel, which was founded as a secondary school or Collège in 1803, when Biel belonged to France.

PROGRESS (1927). First published in *Prager Presse* (October 1927).

THE LYRIC POET. First published in *Prager Presse* (June 1931).

THE WANDERER. First published in *Prager Tagblatt* (October 1928).

I WISH I HAD (1928). First published in *Die literarische Welt* (November 1928).

HARMONY (1930). Unpublished.

CHIVALRIC ROMANCE (1925). First published in *Prager Presse* (February 1933).

OUT OF CONSIDERATION. First published in *Prager Tagblatt* (April 1929).

THE POETESS. First published in *Prager Tagblatt* (April 1933).

THE LUCKY ONE (1928/29). First published in *Prager Presse* (April 1933).

TALE. First published in *Prager Tagblatt* (November 1927).

PROBLEM. First published in *Neue Schweizer Rundschau* (September 1927).

MY FIFTIETH BIRTHDAY (1928). First published in *Prager Presse* (April 1928). The poem's unnamed woman, Walser's female friend from Zurich, also appears in Walser's short story 'Luise' and, as

Klara, in the novels *Der Gehülfe* (The Assistant) (1908) and *Geschwister Tanner* (The Tanners) (1907).

THE LUDICROUS WOMAN (1928/29). First published in *Prager Presse* (May 1930).

THE SONNET OF THE TWIG (1925). First published in *Prager Presse* (February 1928).

DISDAIN IS FUN. First published in *Prager Presse* (February 1926).

WHAT GOT INTO ME? (1927/28). First published in *Prager Tagblatt* (January 1928).

ALONE (1930). Unpublished.

THE MORBID (1930). Unpublished.

POET. First published in *Prager Presse* (May 1930).

SHE WAS BORED (1930). Unpublished.

THE LETTER WRITER (1928/29). First published in *Prager Presse* (March 1931).

THE RAVEN (1928/29). First published in *Prager Presse* (April 1932).

THE SMALL THINGS (1930). Unpublished.

CONTEMPLATION (1930). Unpublished.

THE ADVENTUROUS MOUSE (1930). Unpublished.

IMAGINE HER (1930). Unpublished.

THE PROVEN ONE (1930). Unpublished.

CASTLE ABODE (1930). Unpublished.

WILLING AND ABLE. First published in *Die literarische Welt* (April 1930).

IN THE COUNTRYSIDE (1930). Unpublished.

EASY DOES IT (1930). Unpublished.

LIMITS OF INTELLIGENCE (1930). First published in *Prager Presse* (September 1931).

MY SWEET ONE (1930). Unpublished.

PROUD SILENCE (1930). First published in *Prager Presse* (May 1931).

THE NUN (1930/31). Unpublished.

THE CLUB MEMBER (1930). Unpublished.

THE WOMAN WITH THE FEATHERS (1930). Unpublished.

THE SINGLE WOMAN (1930). Unpublished.

HE WAS NOT NICE (1930). Unpublished.

THE SALESMAN (1931/32). Unpublished.

THE SOPHISTICATED ONE (1931/32). Unpublished.

Who May Say He Knows Existence!

WHO MAY SAY HE KNOWS EXISTENCE! First published in *Wissen und Leben* (June 1925) and reprinted in *Saat und Ernte* (1925).

THE BEAUTIFUL WOMAN FROM THUN (1925). First published in *Die literarische Welt* (December 1925).

WHY THIS ECHO? (1925). First published in *Prager Presse* (July 1932).

LIME BLOSSOM (1925). First published in *Prager Presse* (January 1933).

THE SONNET OF THE CLAWS. First published in *Das Tagebuch* (February 1925).

THE GREEN LAMENTS. First published in *Prager Tagblatt* (August 1925).

THE CREATURE. First published in *Prager Tagblatt* (October 1925).

DO YOU NOT SENSE IT? First published in *Prager Presse* (September 1925).

IT'S HIM, HIM (1925). First published in *Prager Presse* (May 1931).

NUNGESSER. First published in *Prager Presse* (November 1927). Charles Nungesser (1892–1927), French ace pilot and adventurer.

GAME (1930). Unpublished.

ARABIA (1930). Unpublished.

STORY (1930). Unpublished.

IN THE GRAVEYARD (1930). Unpublished.

DO YOU KNOW HER? (1930). Unpublished.

THE NEWSPAPER (1930). Unpublished.

NEW PATHS. First published in *Die literarische Welt* (August 1930).

DREAM (1930). Unpublished.

THE TREES (II) (1930). Unpublished.

THE CASTLE (1930). Unpublished.

I LAY IN BED (1930). Unpublished.

HE WAS FUNNY ONCE (1930). Unpublished.

TIME (II) (1930). Unpublished.

ONCE AND NOW (1930). Unpublished.

THE LADY AT THE PIANO. First published in *Prager Tagblatt* (date unknown).

THE REVENGE SONNET. First published in *Prager Presse* (April 1930).

DELACROIX. First published in *Prager Presse* (October 1930). Eugène Delacroix (1798–1863), French painter and muralist.

THE UNCAPTIVATED. First published in *Prager Presse* (August 1932).

LIFE (1930). Unpublished.

DELETED EARLY POEMS

POEM (pre-1900). Unpublished.

LITTLE DREAM (pre-1900). Unpublished.

UP AND DOWN (pre-1900). Unpublished.

WORLD (II) (pre-1900). Unpublished.

DELETED LATE POEMS

HIS POEMS (1929/1930). Unpublished.

ON A HILL (1929/1930). Unpublished.

SO IT GOES (1929/1930). Unpublished.

SPRING (III) (1929/1930). Unpublished.

SPRING (IV) (1929/1930). Unpublished.

SHE LOOKED PRETTY AGAIN (1929/1930). Unpublished.

Index of Titles